# THE WHOLE DAM STORY

## The Drowning and Rising of a
## River City in the West

### By

### Ella Marie Rast

ISBN: 1-4033-3731-4 (e-book)
ISBN: 1-4033-3732-2 (Paperback)

Library of Congress Control Number: 2002106674


This book is printed on acid free paper.


Printed in the United States of America
Bloomington, IN

1stBooks – rev. 03/08/04

# CONTENTS

# ACKNOWLEDGMENT

I am indebted to the generous and helpful assistance of American Falls Library Staff

Researching Pioneer Journals, Newspaper documentation and individual recollections shows evidence of how the rapidly changing events made a dramatic impact on this corner of southeast Idaho during the past two hundred years. These resources and journals add a unique flavor to what has taken place here. History brings perspective and a depth of understanding from the past to present times. To understand the drive to explore and know the west, we should walk in the shoes of their experience. Freedom and landownership meant a great deal. It was the driving force behind the commitment to make a new life in the wilderness and a burning desire to be free and independent.

I am grateful to have had these resources available, as well as the generous and helpful assistance of American Falls Library Staff.

I especially thank Karen Dismer who willing gave of her editing talents.

I thank the American Falls Historical Society for support and encouragement with this undertaking.

I thank the U.S. Bureau of Reclamation for permission to use archival photographs.

Ella marie Rast

2002

# INTRODUCTION

American Falls is more than a town, or a water fall or a hydroelectric power plant. It is the river, the water and the many people past and present who have wrestled to tame it.

It's story is both ancient and modern. It is a story about changes, centuries old evolving communities by the falls, which is still evolving. In most places along its banks, the high rocky cliffs make access to the Snake River difficult. The story includes native Indian societies, fur trappers, rail roads, cattle barons, pioneers and engineers. It is the drama of how modern dams for irrigation and hydroelectric energy transformed the desert environment and the people who have struggled to make a life here.

Native people had come to understand, how the desert environment worked, and acquired knowledge over the centuries of what was necessary to preserve this fragile space. High desert does provide but it is a fragile balance. With the arrival of wagon trains, the pioneers believed the plains to hold unlimited flora and fauna. While passing through, they were careless and reckless in how they used it. Unknowingly, they upset the delicate natural balance. In a matter of a few years wildlife disappeared on the Snake river Plain, along with the buffalo herds.

In order to appreciate this unique landscape and what has taken place here, whether you are in agreement or in opposition, a peek into the past is necessary.

At one time in the ancient past, the Pacific Ocean virtually lapped against the border of Idaho; it was a tropical environment. As the land masses uplifted and tilted, the coastline gradually moved west 400 miles. During the age of volcanism, rivers were plugged and lakes formed, some of which spilled over causing enormous floods. The Snake River Plain and Yellowstone Geologic Province is a volcanic swath that began to erupt 15 million years ago. The Snake River Plain is believed to be created by a migrating hot spot which is under Yellowstone Park today. More correctly, the continental plate is moving over the hot spot.[1]

These were not exploding volcanos but cracks in the earth's crust allowing lava to ooze out creating a lava desert. Approximately 2000

---

[1] 'Idaho' by John Gottberg

years ago, along the 60 mile Great Rift, the youngest of these flows occurred; it is not considered extinct.

Another cataclysmic event occurred in Idaho, 10,000 years ago, during what is regarded as the second largest flood in the world. Water breached a natural rock dam releasing 20,000 square miles of water from ancient Lake Bonneville. Evidence of 400 foot deep torrents rushing to the Pacific Ocean is found throughout the Portneuf valley and the Snake River Plain, especially the gigantic boulders. The largest examples illustrate waters' awesome power and ability to float objects of this magnitude over long distances.

Geologically speaking, Massacre Rocks is a remnant of an extinct volcano which erupted more than a million years ago and is believed to have been a thousand feet higher than it is at present. Cinders from this ancient volcano are found on the west side of the river and are often fifty feet deep.

Today, the Snake River cuts a swath from east to west across Idaho like a smile, and Sagebrush, a common familiar plant, thrives — able to withstand the conditions of heat, cold and drought.

# CHAPTER ONE

## The SNAKE RIVER PLAIN

The name of this river has nothing to do with snakes although snakes can be found along its banks. Native Americans living along its shores knew the river as 'Shoshone'. The River originates from a gurgling spring in the southern end of Yellowstone National Park in northwest Wyoming. It enters Idaho north of Idaho Falls, where the South Fork and the Henry Fork streams converge, along with others, near Big Springs. With this convergence the mighty Snake River begins winding its way south and west and north and west again tumbling boisterously down one waterfall after another until it reaches Lewiston in northern Idaho where it plunges into the Columbia River to empty into the Pacific Ocean.[2] Early explorers renamed the river, the *Snake* because of the many times this thousand mile river curves back and forth upon it self.

---

[2] Book of Knowledge Encyclopedia

From its origin on the eastern border of Idaho, the river drops at least five thousand feet on its way to the western border of the state at Lewiston. The foaming white waters have roared along canyon walls, past arid landscapes with vigorous energy for thousands of years. Early travelers found the undisciplined river a blessing and a curse, filled with fish and other fauna but often difficult to reach. Any crossing was dangerous.

After purchase of the Louisiana Territory in 1803, President Jefferson had sent out an Expedition, in 1804, with Lewis and Clark in charge, to locate a water route to the Pacific. Knowledge of this region and the Northwest at the time, was scant. The Expedition sparked interest around the world, especially in the fur industry with the lure of high profits. The Pacific Northwest would have been mysterious longer without the incentive for maps needed by trappers. Reliable fur trading routes were necessary if the trappers were to sell the furs. Valuable maps of the region resulted. Long before settlers arrived, both American Falls and the big Buttes were indicated on early maps. One of those maps, used by Sam Houston in 1836, can be seen at the San Jacinto Monument in Texas.

The Overland Astorians, American Fur Trading Company, Rocky Mountain Fur Company, Northwest Fur Company, and British Hudson Bay Fur Company all competed and brought in fur trappers to harvest beaver and mink from Northwest waters. Russian fur trappers had been in region long before and had numerous settlements along the coast.

Russia and Great Britain respected each other as serious contenders in the rich lands west and north of the continental divide. But the new upstart nation, the United States was not given serious consideration.

President Jackson, however, believed the United States had the greatest claim and put in place incentives to encourage permanent settlements, especially in Oregon. As it turned out, the fur trappers accepted a tour of duty but had no serious inclination to settle here in the wilderness. Most of them dreamed of returning to their familiar home land.

By 1820 the level of competition reached serious level. At the time, the United States, a new developing nation, wanted to avoid war. The others also wanted to avoid war since they were far from home base. What the United States lacked in power and resources was offset by the advantage of having a land bridge to transport supplies and people overland. President Van Buren especially understood the strategic importance of avoiding war and proceeded with plans to quickly develop settlements. The first wagon train of settlers set out for Oregon in 1836.

Intent on reaching Oregon, these travelers neither understood nor respected the fragile nature of the high desert; in only a few decades, many species were reduced to alarming numbers and others lost forever.

Nathaniel Wyeth and Captain Bonneville came to the Snake River Plain, in 1832, to trade with the Indians. Wyeth had made a 'Supply Contract 'with the Rocky Mountain Fur Company but when he arrived at "Rendezvous", in 1834, ready to fulfill his promise, to his bitter dismay, the company defaulted! This left him with a large investment in provision filled wagons but no buyers. "Rendezvous" meetings, were social gatherings arranged each year for the benefit of Indians, trappers, and mountain men, The location, in a general way, occurred somewhere around Big Springs or Fort Bridger.

After this disappointment, Wyeth continued west to a point where the Portneuf River enters the Snake River. It was a good location since trails branched off in all directions — to Missouri, California, Oregon, Utah, and Montana — like spokes in a wheel. Seeking revenge and recapture of his investment, he began building a trading post, on July 18, 1834. He sold provisions to Indians and fur trappers. To notify everyone of his allegiance to the new nation, he flew a hand crafted American flag.

That same year, with thirty men, he traveled to British occupied Fort Vancouver and sold his Trading Post to Hudson Bay Company for $8,200, at a loss of $30,000, in retaliation against the Rocky Mountain Fur Company. In 1836, Wyeth returned to the east coast; competition between the two trading companies intensified.

A few years later, wanting to discourage American wagon trains, this British Trading post in Idaho, stopped selling needed supplies to travelers passing through on their way to Oregon. In addition, they freely told frightening stories about crop failure in Oregon and unacceptable weather. Some families abandoned their wagon trains to return east; some settled in 'The Bottoms' near the trading post.

Britain did lose its struggle to control the continent, in 1846, when England divided the Northwest Territory at the 45th parallel, keeping Vancouver Island. Even so, they stubbornly refused to relinquish this Trading Post and continued to harass travelers going west.

Finally, in 1847, the Secretary of War ordered the establishment of an American military fort five miles from the British trading post. The official purpose of Fort Hall being to provide safe travel along the Oregon Trail, while unofficially, intimidating the British to leave was the real goal. It was at this time that the Mormon settlers began to arrive.

Years later, when the Cavalry abandoned Fort Hall, it fell into a ruin known as 'the dobes' by local settlers. Freighting teams, traveling from Utah on their way to Challis, often stopped at the old Fort Hall to salvage whatever they needed to fill an order, perhaps a window or a door for example. The Indians did likewise. At last, there was nothing left to mark the spot of either the Old Fort or the Trading Post.

The famous Lewis and Clark Trail of 1805-1806, lies about three hundred miles north of the Snake River Plain. In 1834, a second scientific expedition organized by Harvard College and the Academy of Natural Sciences of Philadelphia set out following a route further south which later became the Oregon Trail. John Kirk Townsend, a naturalist and ornithologist, and, Thomas Nuttal, a botanist were the scientists in this expedition collecting valuable information of flora and fauna.

In his journal, *'Across the Rockies to the Columbia',* John Kirk Townsend, wrote vivid descriptions of the land and wildlife. His journal relates how survival depended on thoughtful alertness and calm determination while passing through Idaho. His writing opens a delightful window into the past just 200 years ago.[3]

Andrew Henry built the first white shelter along the Snake River, a small fort, near present Rexburg.

---

[3] 'Across the Rockies to the Columbia' by John Kirk Townsend

John Jacob Astor formed the Pacific Fur Company to establish trading posts in the west. He sent out two groups. One group by ship around Cape Horn to build a trading headquarters on the Columbia River.

The other, the William Pierce Hunt party in 1810, Astor sent overland from St. Louis to explore the Rocky Mountain region and to build trading posts. In 1811, the group entered Idaho from Jackson Hole Wyoming. They were the first white men to visit 'at the site of the present city of American Falls. This Astoria-Hunt Party continued to follow the Snake River almost to the Columbia River. Hunt descendants continued to live in southern Idaho.[4]

Later, in 1829, the treacherous 'Thundering Waters' claimed the lives of six American Fur Company trappers who attempted to navigate the falls instead of portaging around. Out of seven men, only one survived. After this tragic accident, trappers referred to it as the American Falls in memory of the lost American Fur Company

---

[4] 'Idaho' by John Gottberg;

trappers. The former picturesque name of 'Thundering Waters' was forgotten.

The waterfall, 'Thundering Waters', had been a sacred site and the location of three Indian villages. This site held great importance for festivals, especially the annual Sun Dance during the moon of falling stars when the tribes requested rain, abundant food and a cure of ills.

Upon the rocky cliffs, in a circular enclosure, with a buffalo head on a center post facing east, the dancers danced. Dancers were required to fast for three days of continual frenzied, dancing. The dancers had no food or water during this time.

At the end of three days, everyone participated in a huge feast.

Being a highly spiritual people, each day begins upon awakening, before facing the sunrise. In preparation for worship, Indians followed a routine of ritual bathing in a stream, both winter and summer. This daily custom was intended to curb indulgence in pleasure. This was a time to greet 'the One who made the land' with prayer and song.

According to native legend, the entire west once was filled with abundant vegetation. As the legend goes, when the people angered the spirits, everything changed. Fire and ash rained down from the heavens and destroyed the land. As a reminder of what had been lost, all that remained was the one hundred mile area to serve as reminder of the Great Spirit's generosity and the admonishment to henceforth be generous and avoid self indulgence.

This lush remnant became sacred ground and belonged to no one; it belonged to everyone. This sacred land was located north of 'Thundering Falls'. The Great spirit charged them to take care of this garden or it would be taken from them. It must be shared and each year allowed to rest.

Another legend tells how the Great Spirit sent mosquitos driving the people and livestock into the hills each summer to allow the grass to grow in peace. Unfortunately, when explorers and cattlemen arrived, finding it vacant claimed this ground for themselves.

Indian culture had no concept of exclusive private ownership since their understanding held that all of the earth had been given as a gift to men by the Spirits. According to custom, visitors had been graciously invited to use the grass land for thousands of years. To be denied access was not a concept that had occurred to them. Later, even after being confined to a reservation, additional parts of the reservation continued to be taken away. The Indians became angry and fearful.[5]

All across the Snake River Plain, the Shoshoni and Bannock Indian tribes lead successful nomadic lives based on horses. Prior to the horse, ample evidence has been found showing they had advanced knowledge of survival skills based on items found in caves. Carbon dating has shown, more than 2000 years ago, they used and stored frozen food.

At first the friendly Indians welcomed newcomers but, as pioneers continued to arrive with increasing numbers of horses and oxen needing food, depleting vegetation and driving out game and buffalo herds, they became fearful. Winter survival for the Indians became very difficult. Earlier, wagon trains had few problems from Indian attacks. In fact, Minerva K. Tiechert, an early settler of the river bottoms, declared, "The Indians mingled with the settlers on the east side of the river and we lived as friends with few disturbances."

---

[5] 'Idaho' by John Gottberg

An early resident of the Snake River bottoms, Johnny Hutchison, explained, "O, there wasn't much to most of the Indian scares stories. Indians plundered and murdered but so did the white man. In 1862, Chief Pocatello wanted the wagon trains to stop because over grazing had depleted vegetation and driven out wildlife.

He also objected to the stench of dead animals along the Oregon Trail, which fouled the air for hundreds of miles. To send a strong message, he attacked a caravan of 200 settlers passing through to Oregon. He burned their wagons and carried away both provisions and livestock. Instead of discouraging the pioneers, the U.S. Cavalry defeated him; he was considered a renegade.

In truth, he was a peaceful leader trying to protect his people, as any leader would. After defeat by the US Cavalry, Chief Pocatello became a familiar character at the Indian Agency. Until his death he remained a respected leader by all who knew him, both Indian and newcomer.

When he died, his unique burial was memorable because his horses were buried with him in a quick sand spring near the falls.

Most attacks on caravans were caused by small disorganized, untrained, teenage parties. In every culture, rebellious young teenagers, want to prove themselves by taking action on their own, eager to show their bravery and toughness'. These youthful parties usually caused more chaos and fear than loss of life.

But, on August 10, 1862, an incident occurred west of American Falls near a rock formation, greatly feared because of its potential for ambush, since only one wagon at a time could pass through the narrow rock notch. Four wagon trains were in the area that day, separated by a few miles.

A small group of Indian youths attacked a small wagon train one half mile east of the rocks, now known as Massacre Rocks, killing two. As these Indians were returning to their camp, they encountered a second group of wagons and killed three men in that attack.

The following day, a third wagon train learned of the attack and sent thirty-five men to do battle with the Indians at Indian Springs where two more men were killed. Altogether, ten men and one girl were buried near huge boulders at Massacre Rocks. The name 'Massacre' was coined around 1920. Although, truly not a massacre, since out of approximately 300 people, eleven people did die. The name stuck. Nevertheless, the name does serve to remind us of the harsh conditions endured by early travelers.

As old stories go, keep in mind that with each telling, stories often get embellished. Some stories, intended to test 'greenhorns', were intentionally exaggerated as part of a prank. Unfortunately, if a 'greenhorn' did not catch on, while getting away from the wild west, he just might repeat the tall tale on his return trip east. All too often, these stories were exaggerated feats of bravery for events that never occurred at all. One old fellow said, "Well, I might have stretched it a bit but, after all, they expected to be entertained!"

# CHAPTER TWO

## Cattle Barons and Settlers

In the West, Cattle Barons had been king since early Territory days. They were their own law and believed since they were the first to claim the land it was theirs to rule. Later as settlers and sheepmen arrived, they considered them to be trespassers and tried to drive them out. And, in fact, held the government in contempt and refused to honor the government's Right to dispense land under the Homestead Act.

The range land was theirs as they saw it. Even when sold, they continued to operate their cattle business as they had always done. The small, scattered farm settlements were at the mercy of the cowboys who cut fences and allowed cattle to forage and trample crops on private land.

The Homestead Act had a long and early history in our nation. Since the Revolutionary War, it had been the practice to give unimproved land to the poor as an opportunity to succeed. Unless improved, land was considered worthless. All that was necessary for a family to acquire a parcel was to file a claim.

Following the Civil War, the South was in financial ruin. In May of 1862, the Homestead Act was again introduced with the intent to offer a new beginning to energetic poor families. However, slave owners hotly objected and debated the issue insisting that "Land must be acquired only by making payment." As a result, the South was excluded from the Homestead Act.

The Homestead offer did apply to other designated areas with certain stipulations. A 160 acres claim could only be granted to a head of family over twenty-one years of age. In addition, while making improvements, the land must be lived upon. Title to the land would be granted if in compliance for five years.

Approximately 600,000 families took advantage of The Homestead Act by going west, between 1862 and 1900. Western climate disappointed many families who learned that 160 acres did not provide enough to sustain a family. If a person chose not to live on the land, he paid $1.25 per acre and required to make improvements before the granting of Title.

The chief beneficiaries of the western land rush were the speculators who sought control of natural resources.

In the late 1880's another Law was passed to encourage the planting of trees. If the homesteader planted a certain number of trees, he would be granted an additional 160 acres. To increase their acreage, many early settlers took advantage of this opportunity. Throughout southeast Idaho, many impressive huge trees can be found that are over one hundred years old, a result of this desert forestation project. The tree planting in the desert only succeeded when planted near streams.

Douglas MacKenzie, a Snake River expedition guide (1818-1821) declared, "This is altogether a delightful country and the American Falls is my favorite camping spot to rest for a few days."

Similar sentiments were expressed in numerous pioneer journals. The trek across southern Idaho was difficult. During the time the wagon trains came through, it would be during the hottest and driest summer months. The fine volcanic soil, quickly, breaks into flour fine powdery dust. The travelers walked in ankle deep dust. They breathed dust. to help dispel the dust, the wagons spread out when possible. Walking was preferred to riding because of the tormenting dust. They never suspected that this torturous desert only needed water to be transformed into green gold.

Imagine yourself as one of these weary, dusty, travelers reaching the American Falls and see the beautiful river of water. Imagine the pleasure of bathing away the dust and resting under the trees near the falls for a few days. Both man and beast needed time to refresh and this was a pleasant place to do it.

The following eloquent journal entry, about the American Falls, by Timothe Lemperit (1848) is so beautifully written, it deserves being shared verbatim since it describes what travelers found at American Falls.

"I admit that the banks of the Snake River create one of the world's most beautiful gateways. I have seen nothing that comes near to it in all my travels up till now. The land is extremely fertile and the vegetation almost continuous. Here there is not the glacial cold we experienced a few days ago."

"The falls or cascades on the Snake River are one of the most beautiful sights in the world, The fall, or drop, is not very great it is true, but what catches the eye is the multiplicity of the streams. We counted up to a dozen of them. It is a veritable flowing staircase. The waters, in great frothy bubbles rushes headlong from one step to the next. At last all this water reaches the great fall which is about thirty feet in height, whereas the others were only from ten to twelve feet high. The rocks that surround the river are all volcanic. We saw several of them that had been hollowed out in the shape of a crater. The last waterfall is more constricted than the others as the free flow of the frothing water is obstructed by two large rocks. The stream thus becomes swifter and more deafening and one has to shout at the top of one's voice to be heard, even to the person standing next to one. There are many other falls on this river but the one I have described is the most beautiful, and the most important. It has been named American Falls. At the foot of the falls are several green islands and these enhance the magnetic charm of a view already most picturesque."

In the late 1800's, the arrival of newspapers represented a sure sign of civilization. Small papers appeared before 1900 with the first three being: The American Falls Boomerang, The Falls Power, and The American Falls Advertiser (1902-1907). In the course of time, one paper would replace another, often in a short time. The American Falls Press (1907-1927) replaced The American Falls Advertiser. Later, the Rockland Times (1910-1917) merged with The American Falls Press to become The Power County Booster (1932-1937). In 1927, The Power County Press arrived and has maintained circulation ever since along with the Aberdeen Times.

Regrettably, few of the original copies are to be found.

# CHAPTER THREE

## Early american Falls

The Idaho Territory was born, in 1863, with the discovery of silver in northern Idaho. The huge Northwest Territory underwent five boundary changes, one of which included the Idaho Territory, before Idaho emerged as the 43rd state, July 3, 1890. The shape of the state is the result of political influence on surveyors to make a mistake since the Canadian border was to have been 200 miles long. As is, the border is only 60 miles in length giving Idaho a unique shape.

Meanwhile, scattered settlements throughout the Territory were dependent upon themselves to maintain law and order. On the banks of the Snake River, at American Falls, a trading community had begun to form, by 1878. Following the closure of Fort Hall, it served as a trading center for cattlemen, travelers and small irrigation companies.

Railroad construction crews arrived at American Falls, in 1883, finding this narrow place in the river attractive for a railroad bridge.

The enterprise spurred growth in the tiny emerging community. It became the major supply distribution point for the railroad. The rough west bank frontier town boasted a hotel, livery stable, store, cafe, saloon and depot as early as 1884.[6]

River crossing from the east side to the westside traders proved an obstacle for customers. In order to retain commercial interests, the town relocated, in 1888, to a forty acre site on the east side, the Riverside Addition, which later would be submerged by the future dam.

During this frontier period, rough trails made travel by wagon difficult indeed. Local ranchers and miners limited these supply trips to twice a year to purchase dried fruit, kerosene, sugar, molasses, honey, lard and flour. These items came in large sized buckets and sacks. With the town now on the east side, those approaching from the west had to overcome the river obstacle. Ferry service below the falls often left customers stranded on both sides.

---

[6] 'Drowned Memories' by Minerva Tiechert

As the little community grew, so did colorful characters. Initially, the promoters were Campbell and Stebbins who sold their interests to Colonel L.L. Evans, a shrewd businessman who succeeded by providing credit to his customers. He presented the customer with an expensive china set, buggy whip or robe when an account was paid in full. His properties were located conveniently across the street from The Depot. He also owned the hotel, the bank and the entire business block. He stocked his general merchandise store with everything from hardware to Indian blankets, overalls, dishes, and groceries.

Goateed, gracious Colonel Evans befriended settlers and Indians with his benevolent concern for their welfare which at the same time promoted his own welfare. And this very fine, courteous, and dignified gentleman acted as though he owned the village — which he did, until a competitor moved in during 1903.

Promoters Greenwood and Philbrick of the Fall Creek Sheep Company, duplicated every service Evans provided. Philbrick's bearing was every bit as regal as Evans. He, too, had a goatee, he befriended the settlers and the Indians, and, — he sponsored young people to college!

Bitter rivalry began. Loyalties were sharply divided. The railroad divided the town between the two rivals with only the Post Office and the Public Office being unaffected. The community benefitted by the competition of two general merchandise stores, two drug stores, two banks, and two water systems. As time went on, the community grew and featured roller skating and three recreation centers: the Odion, the Opera House, the Irene Theater Auditorium. Bands played for dances every weekend.

The river barrier was overcome, in 1904, with the construction of a vehicular bridge, financed largely by the state. The bridge hastened business development in town because west side families could access the market with their product via the railroad at American Falls without needing cross the bridge at Blackfoot. Wagons, pedestrians and horses made the crossing at will, any time of the day or night. Mules, however, refused to set foot on the bridge. Sheep did cross but sheep tend to crowd each other off the bridge. Invariably,

Sheepherders lost a large number of their herd to drowning with each crossing.

Minerva Kohlhepp Tiechert recalled the daily crossing by a teenage girl driving slow plodding oxen across the bridge from the east side to the west for water from the railroad water supply tank. The east side did not have a good water source but the west side of the river had a wonderful spring.

# CHAPTER FOUR

# The INCORPORATION of the CITY

The city fathers were slow to do the legal documentation necessary to be recognized as a city. American Falls had been a vigorous community since the arrival of the railroad in 1883, It had been a viable community since 1870, longer than Pocatello. Perhaps due to local rivalry a common agreement could not reached. Usually, people are eager to to recognized as a legal community. Perhaps, since the town was already on the map, had a railroad, and a post Office, they didn't see the necessity. At any rate, the day came in 1896 when a delegation set off to file the city incorporation papers. To their dismay, they found a legal obstacle, a private party owned the town.

How did this happen? According to legend, after disrupting the town for some time, an undesirable character lost his life in a gun fight. Little was know about the man except that he had a thorough

26

bred horse, a saddle of exceptional fine quality and wore skillfully crafted boots.

The sheriff dispatched a telegraph to his family back east. Upon arrival, his brother impressed the locals as being a gentleman of importance. He seemed an agreeable man and the townspeople, graciously received him into their community.

One day, he chanced to over hear the officials making plans to sign the incorporation documents. Evidently, he saw a golden opportunity and caught the first train out of town to file his own claim.

A few days later, imagine yourself as a member of the delegation, arriving to perform their civic duty, only to learn what had happened a few days earlier. Now a stranger owned the entire city and everything in it. The conversation may have gone something like this.

"I been saying for over eight years, we got to get our town legal. Now we lost our town before we ever got it. He ought to be hung!"

"Are you blaming me? It ain't my fault you buzzard, My wife was bad sick and you know it. You should have done it without me!"

27

"Last year, we gave up too easy when the axle broke in the mud. We just weren't in real hurry to get it done and you all know it. None of figured something like this could happen!"

"The trouble is, we thought we had all the time we wanted."

A sullen silence ensued, pushing back his hat with a gruff cough, "I figure that's what we gotta' do. We can't quit and let the buzzard win. Let's figure out what our next move has to be."

"You're talking crazy! We been hoodwinked by slick bandit and everything is lost, even the new hotel! He out smarted us! About all we can do is string him and I'm all for that notion."

"There ain't a thing we can do about it."

"Now, now cool your spurs! Don't forget we know who he is; he's a city slicker and we can work that to our advantage."

"Yup. And he is back there waiting for us to come home. He already has a plan for us when we get there. What ever he expects us to do, we gotta' make dam sure we don't do that. That might unnerve him."

"You might be right. For sure he will expect us to come back spitting fire!"

"Don't forget, he is smart but he is a greenhorn and doesn't know much. What if we make out to be his friend, treat him real nice."

"Well if that don't beat all for being the dumbest idea I ever heard. He's back there laughing up his sleeve right now. Instead of being 'nice' to him, he needs to be taught a lesson! And I am just the one who can do that. Stealing our town!!"

"You're right there. He does have the upper hand and that is a fact. the law is on his side. None of us want to rot in jail no matter how he has wronged us. This is a high stakes poker game and that's how we got to play it."

Another silence. "He will expect us to come home mad so that is one thing we can't let on to anybody."

"Yup. If we act like nothing happened, he won't know for sure if we know, then he will have to make the first move."

"I have to hand it to you. We can have some fun playing him along. I kinda' like the sound of this."

"One of us should be his friend. Who is going to volunteer to be his best friend?"

Silence. "Come on now, one of us has to do it. Its easy duty. Have supper with him. Take him fishing. Get him to trust you. Remember, out of curiosity, he is going to be fishing for information, too."

"I'd rather strangle his neck! I sure as hell don't want to eat with him."

"I don't fancy being a friend to that scoundrel but it just might work. I'm a prudy good story teller, if I do say so myself. Once his guard is down, I'll tell him the story about Tex and Johnson, and I'll make sure it is real entertaining for him. When he learns how bad we treat strangers that do us wrong, in American Falls, he'll be ready to shit his pants. Recalling his tall tales, the men nodded as chuckles rippled around the table. When details were worked out the meeting adjourned for the long trip home.

The group returned from Malad and causally went about their business as though nothing unusual had happened. As agreed, one of the men began an offer of friendship and as the days passed, the stranger accepted an invitation to go fishing. The day could not have been finer, with blue skies and a gentle breeze to soothe the spirit. By mid afternoon, the story telling had begun. The stranger was surprised to learn about the raw justice still being practiced in the region and visibly shocked by the hanging of Tex and Johnson from the railroad bridge.

The stage had been set. He changed the subject. "Have you heard the rumor going around town?"

"Why, no can't say I have. What sort of rumor?"

"Well, the way I hear tell, some fellers are real pissed at somebody and are planning to take the law into there own hands by arranging a neck tie party. It might just be rumor but I sure don't want to miss it. Don't know the particulars — you heard anything?"

"No, I haven't?"

"Well, if you ever wanted to see a hanging, you might get your chance real soon. that bunch is wanting swift justice at the railroad bridge."

The gentleman's face blanched, knowing he was the man in question; his enthusiasm for fishing waned.

"Are you alright? You're looking a mite peaked."

Suddenly nauseated, the gentleman answered, "It must be the sun. I need to lie down, I'm going back to the Hotel to rest so I can join you later." Upon returning to his room, he hastily packed his bags and caught the next train out of town never to be heard from again.

Patiently, just in case the man returned to assert his claim, the committee waited the legal ten years before attempting to file their papers a second time. The incorporation documents were duly filed, July 11, 1906, and American Falls became an official Idaho city as the following newsclip testifies:

American Falls became a legal incorporated City on July 11th, 1906 at Malad, Idaho according to letters of incorporation granted to the village of American Falls.

Otis W. Dutro presented a Petition with 25 taxpayer resident signatures. Sixty of the total 360 residents were certified taxpayers. Trustees of the village were: J.L. McKnown, R.B. Greenwood, Alonzo Roberry, Ottis W. Dutro and T.E. St. John.

The original town site papers were dated 1896 but were not filed until 1906.


One of the first laws enacted by the new citizens was to establish American Falls officially as a "dry" town. The west side of the river was outside their jurisdiction so liquor flowed freely. Under these circumstances, enforcing the law proved challenging for the sheriff. Sober citizen traveled across the river only to stagger home later the same day.

Many amusing anecdotes occurred. Here is one: The alert American Falls sheriff discovered something suspicious one day as he surveyed the depot loading platform. He noted that right there in plain view, someone had "innocently hidden'" three barrels of whiskey among the other legal barrels and cartons on the loading dock.

Fearing that good citizens in 'his dry town' might have chosen a life of crime; the honest sheriff posted a guard. Several days passed without any attention being paid to the whiskey barrels. However, a few days later, upon closer investigation, to his dismay and right under the nose of the guard, a sly villain had crept underneath the dock, drilled holes into the barrels from below and drained all three barrels![7]

---

[7] 'Idaho State Journal' by Bertha Sawyer

# CHAPTER FIVE

# ISLAND POWER PLANT AND HOME

As Idaho entered the 20th century, hydroelectric energy was the new exciting technology. The first electric plant in the northwest to transmit power ten miles was at Oregon City, Oregon. The first plant built in idaho supplied power to mines at Silver City. The second plant, located at American Falls began construction on the Island Power plant, in 1901. Construction was difficult because at first, there was no access to the island except from the railroad bridge overhead. Workers carried construction materials over the railroad ties and then down a ladder to the island. As work progressed a foot bridge was constructed from the east side, and later, a wide mule foot bridge on the west side.

In 1902, operation began under the management of Charles Johnson. The building itself was drafty, cold and extremely noisy. The gearing made a ripping, roaring racket and, in addition, when used for peak demand, the 60 horse gas fired engine noise could be heard miles away.

The plant produced electricity twenty four hours a day. According to Charles Johnson, "We used to start about an hour before sunrise and quit an hour after sun up, a comfortable shift for a man. We controlled the turbine speed by hand, readjusting for every change of load. Hand rheostats regulated the voltage. Voltage regulators were unknown and water wheel governors were only a curiosity. Open knife switches, excitor switches, rheostats voltmeters and ammeters were mounted on a wooden frame.

"The hand operation of high tension switches, required crossing the river and climbing a pole to reach the switches, a hazardous duty especially during a blizzard. When a head gate got blocked with ice, it took the muscle of four men, along with chopping through ice, to move the head gate. Sometimes, to keep turbines moving and get liquid moving again, it might be necessary to chop a channel through the ice.

"Sometimes, we wrapped a man in a slicker and pushed him through the manhole cover on a turbine casing so he could use hoes and shovels to clear the ice. Once cleared, the water would again be put through the turbines.

"The power company slogan, *"Uninterrupted Service"*, was intended to prove our service was superior to steam. It was intended to promote user confidence. Under the circumstances, this was not easy to do," according to Johnson.[8]

Three plant operators received salary of $60.00 per month, an excellent wage at the time. The plant produced 1500 kilowatts. The generating plant was located in the basement of the building. Since Mr. Johnson's children had no yard to play in outdoors, he often brought his toddlers down into the plant to play. The men taught them all about turbines, switchboards, meters, and generators.

. Another benefit of employment included the use of a horse named Fritzi and a single seat buggy. Johnson's duties also included being lineman. Sometimes he would take his children along when he worked. He hitched up Fritzi early in the morning, took along a picnic basket filled with good things to eat and drove to Bannock Creek to meet the lineman from Pocatello, who patrolled on

---

[8] 'Legacy of Light' a History of Idaho Power Company by Susan Stacy

horseback. A telephone line had been strung with the power line. When a problem was discovered the lineman simply climbed the pole and used the private line to report the trouble to the plant with instructions to shut off the electricity so the line could be repaired.

The Island plant provided electrical power to Pocatello, Blackfoot and American Falls.

To meet increasing demand for electric power, a second Power Plant was built on the west bank. Electric use in those early days consisted of bare, 16 candle watt, carbon filament bulbs dangling from the ceiling. Although feeble, the electric light was better than kerosene lamps. Public confidence in electricity was slow to develop. To increase demand for electricity, marketing strategies were implemented. A highly skilled, helpful staff was retained by the Idaho Power Company to assure customer satisfaction and to assist all electric users with their problems. A huge success, the strategy focused primarily on the needs of agriculture and the housewife.

One of the benefits for the plant manager included having living quarters for his family in the power plant building. His family lived there in this unusual setting from 1902 until 1917. The island home came with a few special features not found in most homes at the time. It was surrounded by the soothing sound of flowing water, had a spectacular view from the upper floor and electricity supplied by whirling generators. The rooms were kept cozy using Electric heaters designed by Mr. Johnson himself.

Many envied the home for its spacious front room, three bedrooms, and indoor bathroom. The bath water had to be heated on the kitchen stove which was not electric. Laundry equipment consisted of a washboard, tub and boiler. Mrs. Johnson hung the clothes outside to billow in the wind on a forty foot wooden platform along side the house. Since she insisted on having a garden to raise vegetables and flowers, a 12 by 20 foot form was filled with soil from the east bank of the river.

Life in the stone house was considered to be the life of an aristocrat but Mrs. Johnson never felt completely safe living on the edge of the dangerous swirling white water; one wrong step could mean sudden death. The small platform afforded limited space for children to play.

Thundering coal burning locomotives roared directly overhead with clanging bells and loud whistle blasts. As it galloped along, the house shuddered as did the bridge. Soot rained down on wash day soiling Mrs. Johnson's freshly washed clothes hung out to dry. Seemingly one behind the other, numerous freight trains and six passenger trains whizzed by overhead each day.

As plant superintendent, Mr. Johnson loved people and often entertained. A dinner invitation from the Johnson's was considered being put a bit above the rest of society. An excellent cook, Laura Johnson cooked on a wood burning range, baking delicious pastries in her oven. She specialized in Danish dishes and always won blue ribbons at the Fair. Compared to her breads, bakery products seemed tasteless. She kept herself busy baking for family and friends. Their home also served as a boarding home for teachers, stenographers, and laborers.

When another child was expected after fifteen years of living in this home, Laura insisted it was time to move to McKinley Street.

Without regrets she left the stone river house. However, the children cherished their unusual life in the middle of the river.

Laura worried when her oldest child, Bill age five, started school. She feared he might slip into the river on the way home. Had she known what his daring spirit was willing to do she would have died at an early age herself. Above the roaring waters, he would dangle by his knees from railings. On dares, he would dive into the deepest pools with lungs bursting, and grab mud from the total darkness to prove he had reached bottom.

Despite their adventures, the Johnson children grew up. Bill and Charlie went on to medical School, Mot entered the art field, Pete went to New Zealand as a missionary, and Lillian married Bernie Meuhlen.

The stone house on the island has been vacant now for many years and been declared unsafe. Its' scheduled demolition never occurred, much to the delight of romantics. The building is a familiar, scenic landmark. Sadly, the windows are broken and every year more shingles fly away. As a historical building, it needs a new roof.

Without attention, one sad day this local landmark will become a pile of rubble and wash away.

Until the Second World War, when it was removed as a security measure, a swinging pedestrian bridge connected the house with the west bank. Walking suspended over the foaming white water was an exiting adventure, especially for youngsters. It is missed by all who knew it.

# CHAPTER SIX

# PEOPLE from the EARLY DAYS

Minerva K Tiechert left an invaluable resource about the early days along the river near American Falls, where she recorded her observations in a book, '*Drowned Memories*'. Besides being an author she also had a reputation as an artist.

She knew the region intimately since this is where she grew up and watched history take place. She said, "Grandma Elizabeth West was one of the few women living in the region during those early years around 1880. Strange how primitive we lived, most of us in log cabins with dirt roofs and handmade latches on the door! If fortunate, we had an old rag rug to cover the bare dirt floor.

"When Annie West moved to The Bottoms with her three pretty dark eyed daughters, she found few women, but there were many suitors for her daughters. I shall always remember the laughing eyes of Annie West and her beautiful daughters which are representative of an earlier generation and oh, how Annie loved to dance!

"In the days of the cattle barons, dances were held in log houses and music furnished by cowboys with accordion, mouth organ, or banjo. Beautiful dresses were made in Saint Louis or New York and shipped to Idaho for the dances. The young ladies changed dresses as often as three times during an evening. Sometimes a hint of luxuries from the folks back east would reach us such as chocolates put up in silver papers with perfume balls between the papers.

"We danced until the wee hours and the cowboys made many a good natured rush for the girls before they played, *Home Sweet Home!*" No man smoked in the presence of a lady. and any drunken man was hustled out. Ninety percent were from the south and that may account for the gallantry and hospitality associated with folks from 'The Bottoms'. The kinder hospitality we knew then, was free from caste or personal ambition. It put people at a higher plane than now. "Tis true there were sinners, then as now. I wonder," asked Minerva, "Is it men or is it women who have lost respect for ladies?"

Names associated with The Bottoms from 1838 to 1920 include Campbell and Stebbins, the I.L. Ranch, the Muleshoe Ranch, the High and Stout Outfit who bought out the Fisher Outfit and Texas cattleman, John Sparks who ran 70,000 head of cattle on a range from Utah to Montana in summer range and wintered at the east bottoms.

Between 1885 and 1891, the cattle business suffered great losses due to drought and weather. The range had been over grazed and could not sustain large herds under drought conditions. Under normal desert conditions forty five acres of open range, were required to support one steer. Suddenly, instead of 38,000 calves to represent a year of work, they could only harvested 60. Where as they had believed, the cattle business was the only suitable business for this region. With in just a few years, the severe weather conditions quickly brought them to ruin. They had resented farmers. They had not appreciated irrigation held a potential benefit for them since cattlemen had been accustomed to using all land without any investment.

Persons who predicted a brighter future for the desert with water were considered dreamers. Surveys and locations for irrigation systems were plotted in the latter part of the century but it was the Carey Land Act of 1894 which financed irrigation projects allowing the transformation of the desert to became a reality. Small projects were scattered here and there but the first large project resulted with the construction of the Milner Dam. In March of 1905 at Twin Falls, the first water began to flow through canals. Perrine and Ribblet proved to be strong advocates for the benefits of irrigation projects. Frank Ribblet, historian and engineer, was the first to conceive the practicality of using water from American Falls to augment the water supply needed to irrigate the desert downstream.[9]

As it is, within one year 300,000 acres of land had been cleared of sagebrush and was producing tomatoes, beans, fruit, wheat and potatoes. The Snake River Valley was being transformed from a desert into the garden spot of the world, 'the Nile of Idaho'. The Magic Valley.

Even so, upstream, before the irrigation systems were firmly in place, early farmer settlers living outside the perimeters of the 'The Bottoms', found that life was harsh indeed and 160 acres would not support a family. Limited river crossings to obtain needed supplies

---

[9] 'Six Decades Back' by Charles S. Walgamott

and services made it difficult to reach market. In 1890, Blackfoot gained respect from settlers with the construction of a bridge, a grist mill and a lumber yard. Prior to that they had to travel to McCammon or Eagle Rock (Idaho Falls) in order to bring home flour. American Falls had not developed much beyond being a trading post before the railroad arrived in 1882.

Frontier life attracted bad characters as well as hard working people looking for a new honest life. The village of American Falls had a reputation as a tough community. With the railroad more elements were added to the diversity of village life. North of Malad, Idaho, there was no law. Law abiding citizens were expected to take the law into their own hands and not bother the sheriff at Oxford. Sometimes the wrong people decided to become the law resulting in a temporary reign of terror.

Back in 1882, as construction of the Railroad bridge over the Snake River had begun, two men were hanged from beams of the new structure. Mrs. Watts, who was a witness, related the story to Mary Hunter.

"Tex and Johnson were gamblers, robbers, horse thieves and gunmen. The village had been subjected to a reign of terror. Territorial Law officers were days away. One night, after having been to the Saloon, Tex and Johnson entered the Oliver Boarding House which was full so men were sleeping on the lobby floor. For sport, and without remorse, they shot toes off a sleeping guest, and then laughed at their victim. The people in the community were enraged and agreed these men had to be stopped. The next day a determined committee caught them by surprise in the saloon, and ordered the two to leave town and never come back. They left town.

Once power has been tasted, it is often difficult to let go. The next day they boldly rode back into town and announced their defiance and intention to stay. Two chinese railroad workers had been found murdered and these two were the primary suspects. Tired of Tex and Johnson, the folks formed a vigilante committee which grimly entered the Saloon. Johnson pulled his gun and began shouting and firing; Tex used a chair to bat heads. Somehow, Tex got tangled up in the broken furniture and fell, breaking his right arm. Quickly the two outlaws found themselves subdued and escorted, protesting and pleading, to the new span of the Oregon Short Line Railroad Bridge.

Tex and Johnson found they were the featured guests at a neck tie party organized by the committee and were quickly fitted with rope nooses for the hanging. Tex objected to being hung with an old rope and jumped off onto the rocks below, yelling, "I'll be in hell ten minutes before you get there." Johnson desperately pleaded for his life, promising to change his ways. But, according to custom, after a short wait for the usual last words, he, too, was hurried into eternity. He managed to grab the edge of the bridge with his fingers for a little while as he pleaded for mercy. The vigilantes reminded him he had had his chance but had not shown mercy to others.

According to *The American Falls Advertiser*, "His body swung back and forth over the foaming water, the spray wetting his high heeled boots and leather chaps". Thus ended a page in the book of Frontier Law. The memory faded. Years later, workers repairing the bridge, discovered a skeleton near the spot the hanging is believed to have taken place.[10]

The moral of this story is, 'Mind your manners in American Falls, or else!'

The first place to provide meal service in American Falls was established by Ed Keane, in 1883. It was located three doors from The Oliver House. All too often certain customers disrespected the proprietors services. One day, when band of tough Montana horse thieves passed through town, they enjoyed a hot meal, but then tossed the dishes in the air and shot them into pieces!

At the time, the cattleman, Sparks, had his base camp on the Snake River Bottoms. Rustling caused high losses and he wanted to end the problem but without doing the dirty work himself. He caught a cowpoke named Paxton changing the brand on his cattle. Since people were expected to take the law into their own hands and not

---

[10]

bother the sheriff at Oxford, had he hung Paxton for rustling, it would have been an accepted action. Instead, John Sparks went to American Falls and hired Jackson, a no-good gunslinger, to kill Paxton.

Jackson accepted the job, but being a coward he looked for an easy way out. He started out by pretending to be Paxton's friend. The two drank together all day. Paxton was too drunk to walk when they went to dinner. Still he did not shoot him, it was only while they were eating that he stood up and shot him in the head. With the posse in pursuit, he galloped south never to be heard from again.

An early settler of this era, Liberty Hunt, lived at Gifford Springs near Minidoka. Liberty would come to American Falls with his wagon team to buy supplies. After stabling his horses, he would spend the evening dining in West's Saloon. The next day, to reach the stores, he walked across the river on the railroad bridge. After completing his purchases, he enlisted the help of Chinese or Japanese porters to help carry his heavy supplies across the river on the railroad ties of the bridge to his wagon. If a train came along, the only thing they could do was slip under the bridge, balancing themselves on the beams underneath the tracks while the train rolled by over head showering them with hot sparks. It is a wonder they could clamber back up still carrying their heavy burdens. It might involve carrying six 100 pound sacks of horse feed in addition to the other food stuffs.[11]

The early days of the Idaho Territory were primarily settled by families taking advantage of the Homestead Act. Cattlemen continued to use the open range and any farm in their path without payment until around 1920. Having ruled the west for several decades, the cattlemen were accustomed to having their way. The men they employed as cowboys, not surprisingly, emulated their bosses, and had a reputation for being wild and unruly when they came to a town. Being survivors of harsh range life, they believed they had earned this right. They, too, felt an arrogant disregard for Law and Order except as it suited them. Upon leaving town, a trail of destruction usually followed their departure. The modern western romance novel has its roots in this period.

---

[11] 'Welcome to Main Street American Falls Idaho' by American Falls Chamber of Commerce

On July 3rd, 1890, the cowboys were in American Falls enjoying rest and recreation time from the trail life. This was also the time that Idaho became the 43rd state, with a celebration at the new capital, Boise, an event preceded by much publicity. The tireless work of Fred T. Dubois made statehood possible; had his efforts failed, Idaho would have been annexed to Washington and Nevada. He, also, persuaded Washington D.C. to allow the signing of the documents on July 3rd, instead of the official date the 4th, so that the 43rd star would be placed on the flags that year, a year earlier than it would otherwise have been.

With so much publicity, people in southeast Idaho lamented that no part of the celebration would be happening in the eastern part of the state. The cowboys especially saw this as a missed opportunity to take part in a really big celebration and they did like to celebrate when they were in town!

All trains going west and east stopped at American Falls to refill steam engine water boilers. On this particular day, during the water stop the cowboys discovered entertainments, enroute to Boise, were on board. The ornery cowboys saw their chance and fearlessly, at gunpoint, ordered the engineer off the train. They persuaded the musicians, at gunpoint, onto the station platform to conduct a command performance for the pleasure of the cowboys. When satisfied, the train proceeded to its destination. Since the musicians arrived late, they were not allowed to perform and therefore were not paid! Together with the frightening gunpoint experience, no official performance and no payment, it has to be said, 'The musicians had a really bad day.'

A truly typical western character was 'Doc' West, a former cowboy, who joined Walter Oliver in the saloon business until prohibition when, being strongly patriotic, he operated a 'dry' saloon because whatever the Law, he supported it. Civic minded, he organized a baseball team in American Falls and sponsored many other movements. Known by all as a decent man of fine character while at the same time being a fearless and outspoken individual.

According to B.W. Davis, "In 1916 he was elected sheriff but died before he could take office. His funeral was something to remember. People came from Ogden, Salt Lake, Idaho Falls, Pocatello and other places. Church people, all kinds of business people, Indians, cowboys, doctors, dentists, lawyers, teachers, and people from every class you can imagine."

An early resident, Alta Stanger explained, "Indians wore braids down their backs and big floppy hats. Every Indian had their own blanket. Sometimes they would camp near the river. I never knew them well, I felt squeamish about meeting them face to face because of what I had been told as a child. I would listen to them talk, even though I could not understand a word.

"I rode to High School on horseback. A lady had to look like a lady whether she rode a horse or not. So, to solve the problem, I pinned up my skirt, donned a divided riding skirt. When I got to school, I unpinned my skirt, took off the divided skirt and arrived looking like a proper lady. My classmates teased me saying, 'When you come off that horse, you look like a fashion plate!'

"Dances were different in those days; everybody was your partner and you got acquainted with all kinds of boys. It was a good clean custom and we all had fun. Other popular activities included church, school plays, traveling circuses and the Chataqua which brought in wonderful actors and educational speakers. When the Negro Troupes came into town, we were thrilled because they were so funny.

"We had a beautiful auditorium in town where lots of good entertainment came through town and was attended by elite people We common folk were afraid to go among those well dressed people.

"Because of my brothers, who were Rodeo performers with records, I attended rodeos. All they ever got for their efforts were ribbons.

""During those early days, American Falls was a rough place and people were being killed. One famous outlaw made an impression on me, Diamond Field Jack. He was wealthy because he robbed trains and anything else he could find."

Jackson Davis, Diamond Field Jack, and Lava Jack — may be some of the many names of a well know figure in those early days. In the spring of 1894, a pleasant young man with the manners of a cowboy rode onto the Snake River Plain. Described as companionable, kindhearted and fond of children. He talked of finding gold and diamonds and was confident one day he would be wealthy. Accurate with his gun if he deemed it necessary, he was feared and respected. He worked for cattlemen and got involved in a dispute with sheepmen over the use of grazing land which the cattlemen claimed sole right to use. Cattlemen did not share with sheepmen. February 1896, he was accused of murdering two sheepherders. He was arrested and found guilty but two hours before his hanging he received a Stay of Execution and eventually an unconditional pardon. In 1936, he was believed to live in Los Angeles. He was a gambler and perhaps he lost his fortune. Anyway, for many years during the thirties and forties, a ragged, fierce looking, prospector with a long white beard lived in a log cabin beside the lava cliffs along the Snake River where he panned for gold. On rare occasions Lava Jack came into American Falls for supplies with his mule, always carrying a rifle. He would tie his mule to the hitching rail behind the mortuary. Is this embittered recluse Diamond Field Jack? Whether Lava Jack is the Diamond Field Jack of legend is for you to ponder.[12]

About this time in history, a hard hitting frontier character described as a female outlaw owned a gold mine, the 'Golden Slipper' near Neeley. Although a staunch Catholic, she did not hesitate to cuss. Smarter than heck, when she spoke, people stopped to listen. She carried words as her weapon of choice and when she aired her views, she drew large crowds and brilliantly moved people to agree with her opinions. Generally Irish Mary Franklin did not carry a gun but was known as a dead shot.

One of the most amazing citizens early American Falls had. Her home, though, was a shack which locals described as a place you would not want to pen your chickens. Despite that, she was a sought after housekeeper and with her training as a midwife, she delivered hundreds of babies in the area.

---

[12] Idaho Handbook by Don Root

When the Banks locked their doors, Irish Mary used her pistol to convince the banker of the Evan State Bank to return her money. He handed over her money without much argument because of her reputation with a gun was not a bluff.[13]

Another lady deserving respect as a business woman in a frontier town was Marguerite Wilson owner of the Log Cabin Cafe. The town attracted a rough element but she was up to the task. If anyone caused too much trouble in her cafe she might use a broom stick on them and when necessary she could toss them out bodily by herself. when the town relocated, so did her Log Cabin Cafe delicious, plain meals. Without her generosity, many people would have gone hungry."[14]

Rumors about dam construction at American Falls circulated around Illinois, in 1898. On the strength of what he heard, Charlie

---

[13] Main Street American Falls Idaho

[14] Main Street American Falls

Thornhill came to find work here! Of course the reports were false. In Neeley, he met his future wife Gertrude and felt the trip had been for a reason. He opened an Ice Business. Four miles up river from the falls, lay Horse island, with a spring-fed lake, Horseshoe Lake. Here he harvested ice in blocks or cakes 12 by 16 inches weighing 200 pounds during the winter and stored the ice under 24 inches of sawdust in a building on the island. All year he delivered ice to meat markets, drug stores, grocery stores and homes.

Ice harvesting was a tricky operation since it took three trips with an ice saw across the ice to cut one block deep enough to remove. He worked with a horse and bobsled to haul the ice.

After the construction of the dam had been completed, his business went under water. But not his determination. He built an ice manufacturing plant in town and continued ice delivery until his services lost favor to the convenience of the electric refrigerator. Once again, he adapted by setting up 500 Cold Storage lockers and a meat wrapping service for the convenience of farmers after fall butchering. He also sold ice cream.[15]

Businessmen of American Falls were confident the town had a future because they believed the Falls Irrigation District would soon be funded, making water available for irrigation. Water would create boon for the area.

By chance, on February 4, 1912, O.S. Baum visited J.V. Dawson in Gooding Idaho who introduced him to I. Bert Perrine. In 1892, Congress had sent Perrine to Idaho to do an irrigation feasibility study at American Falls. He spoke favorably of the town of American Falls and was enthusiastic about the future possibilities for southern Idaho when irrigation projects were funded. His farm at Blue Lakes demonstrated he understood his topic.

A few days later, February 8th, Baum visited American Falls himself; he returned February 12th, 1912, to set up his law practice. In less than eight days after first learning of American Falls, he had

---

[15] 'the Fiftieth Anniversary Issue of Power County Press'

become a resident. Baum's friendship with Perrine continued.
Perrine continued to argue the positive benefits of a "Big Dam" at
American Falls. Throughout the summer of 1912, many conferences
were held regarding irrigation at Neeley and Michaud Flats but the
major benefactors would be the Magic Valley farmers. Pleasant
Valley was never considered for irrigation.[16]

---

[16] 'Saga of the American Falls Dam by Irvin Rockwell

# CHAPTER SEVEN

# The IDAHO POWER STORY

The history of electricity had a slow beginning with experimentation since 1600. With the invention of the telegraph, practical electrical inventions began to appear. Edison invented the stock ticker in 1869, the phonograph in 1877. He worked out the principle of the incandescent light bulb, in 1879, after which there was no stopping this new technology.

The first successful transfer of electricity occurred, in 1890, from Oregon City to Portland, Oregon, a distance of twenty miles. This event sparked interest everywhere, especially in the west with great distances and sparse populations.

1900 marked the beginning of construction of a 900 kilowatt hydroelectric facility near Kuna, Idaho. In 1901, this plant sent the miracle of electricity via a 22,000 volt transmission line to the Silver City mines. Electricity transformed the operation of heating buildings and lighting the mines, as well as powering trolleys and equipment.

From 1903 to 1910, the Trade Dollar Mine produced $30 million dollars of gold.

Nampa, Caldwell, and Boise communities quickly showed an interest in electricity. When O.G. Markhus developed the first electric irrigation pump to lift water directly out of the river, the farmers, too, became interested because this invention opened the possibility of irrigating land that had been inaccessible because of cliffs. In this small way the hydroelectric company became involved in both the business of making electricity out of water and also selling irrigation water to farmers.

In 1901, the American Falls Light and Water Company opened its first electric plant but in 1905, the name changed to American Falls Power Company. Next, to meet increasing demand, in 1907, the American Falls Water Power Steam Plant opened a steam plant in Pocatello.

The increasing costs of operations required the Idaho Power Company to promote usage of appliances not yet invented in order to be a profitable business.

Electricity is mysterious. Although not understood, we accept it because it works. Idaho Power company took a leadership position unique in the business world. The company sought to provide, service and develop what customers required. A rapidly changing business, it required increasing investments to access improved technology. Competition was ruthless.

To avoid duplication and reduce costs, Companies began to consolidate and merge. During 1913 and 1914, a financial crisis occurred which resulted in the Idaho Power Company corporate office being relocated to Maine. This decision was reversed in 1989. Because the Idaho Snake River Territory is huge, William Wallace, general manager of Idaho Power Company recognized the importance of uniting the fragmented districts. Each electric district represented diverse interests such as mining, industry, and agricultural interests. To create unity, he created four divisions, Pocatello, Twin Falls, Boise, Payette, with four managers. In 1920, 'the Electrikat', a monthly magazine was first published.

## Electricity Sonnet to Every Housewife

How can I serve the?  Let me count the ways.

I'll serve the well at morning, noon, and night.

By chilling all thy foods to keep them right,

so thou canst serve them with delight and grace.


I'll serve the to the level of every day's

Most quiet need for heat and cheering light.

I'll serve the cleanly, putting dirt to flight.

I'll serve the quickly in a hundred ways.


I'll serve the with a power put to use

In washing clothes and dishes, and in cleaning house.

And as thou come to put upon me greater tasks

I shall but serve the even better still.


...by P.K.D.  Printed in 'Electrikat'

A woeful lack of guidelines and operating procedures created problems due to major deferred maintenance. In addition, Pocatello and Twin Falls had a surplus of energy, while Boise had a shortage. To add to the difficulties, in 1913, the Public Utility commission froze the rate schedules of all electric companies. Prior to this ruling, fierce price cutting competition had, unfortunately, been taking place The electric companies found themselves locked into rates below their costs.

Not until after the war, would a request to raise rates to a realistic price be granted by the legislature. Duplicated equipment was eliminated when Mr. Wallace connected Twin Falls to the western area of Idaho. By 1916, all of the combined plants could generate 21,240 kilowatts. But, the debt of the merged companies exceeded the value of the plants.

In amount of $6.7 million dollars, on January 2, 1917, Idaho Power invented the 'open-end Mortgage'. The idea of borrowing money in that amount astonished the public. Actually, this transaction did increase the value of the company. Idaho Power earned itself the reputation of being an independent company since the company had always resisted offers from federal licensing and government agencies.

To increase revenues for the company, the Idaho Power Company launched a marketing program using trained employees to promote the benefits of new electrical appliances. Idaho Power Company listened and was ahead of the industry developing electric stoves, refrigerators, vacuums, washing machines, clothes dryers, and water heaters. The Idaho farm Water heater became popular throughout the world for its convenience.

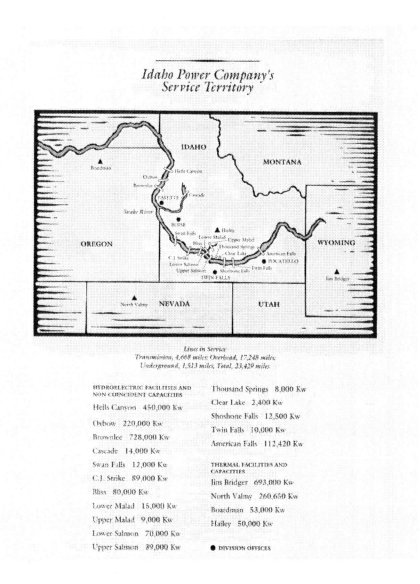

**Idaho Power Company's Service Territory**

Lines in Service
Transmission, 4,668 miles; Overhead, 17,248 miles;
Underground, 1,513 miles, Total, 23,429 miles.

HYDROELECTRIC FACILITIES AND NON-COINCIDENT CAPACITIES

Hells Canyon  450,000 Kw
Oxbow  220,000 Kw
Brownlee  728,000 Kw
Cascade  14,000 Kw
Swan Falls  12,000 Kw
C.J. Strike  89,000 Kw
Bliss  80,000 Kw
Lower Malad  16,000 Kw
Upper Malad  9,000 Kw
Lower Salmon  70,000 Kw
Upper Salmon  39,000 Kw
Thousand Springs  8,000 Kw
Clear Lake  2,400 Kw
Shoshone Falls  12,500 Kw
Twin Falls  10,000 Kw
American Falls  112,420 Kw

THERMAL FACILITIES AND CAPACITIES

Jim Bridger  693,000 Kw
North Valmy  260,650 Kw
Boardman  53,000 Kw
Hailey  50,000 Kw

● DIVISION OFFICES

The marketing focus shifted to the housewife's need for relief from her heavy work load, in particular, the weekly laundry. She had to carry and heat fifty gallons of water just for one laundry day. In

69

addition, she had to scrub clothes on a wash board, boil the heavily soiled clothes and carry the wet wash outside to dry. It was back breaking work. The laundry still had to be taken down, folded and ironed. Not yet finished, she still had to carry all the water back outside and dump it somewhere. Monday was washday, Tuesday was ironing.

The invention of the washing machine was a boon. And, the "Hot Point Iron" eliminated the use of cast iron versions which had to be heated on the stove; in the summer heating the wood stove in order to iron was a hot unpleasant chore. Its popular competitor, the gas iron was highly dangerous and caused many burns and house fires.

I remember my father refusing to allow my mother to purchase a gas iron because he feared for her safety. He had no objection to an electric iron.

Up until the 30's, women had stubbornly resisted using the electric stove because they were accustomed to the convenience of the attached water tank found on wood stoves. This single factor was significant on wash day. Work to develop an electric hot water heater began.

In 1935, the Idaho Power Company sold more appliances than any other electric company. In 1935, this company also won an award for outstanding contribution to the development of electric light and electric power for the convenience of the public.[17]

---

[17] Legacy of Light', A History of Idaho Power Company... Susan M. Stacy

# CHAPTER EIGHT

# THE RAILROAD STORY

The Oregon Short Line Railway contract to relocate and raise roadbed to a one and one half percent grade was approved. This meant raising the railroad bridge twenty one and one- half feet above its prior elevation and at least thirty one feet higher near the river.

Mr. Swinburn of Applegate Construction built the new railroad grade through American Falls beginning, March 1925. He stated, "My company expects to complete the job in six to eight months. It will employ sixty to eighty men and move 260 cubic yards of dirt per day".

By June 25, 1925, the Applegate Construction Company bridge crew had reached the point where the big railroad bridge started its upward climb. A big steam shovel cut through to the new townsite. Each day, two trains of 12 cars hauled dirt to the large fill just north and east of the high school. Crews handled the work on the deep fill at the rate of 100 or more feet a day. Besides the new grade approach, it is necessary to raise up a new bridge on nine tower piers. The single track main line bridge will be 77 feet above the water at its highest point. The total weight of steel trusses to be 1220 tons.

The piers must be extended an additional 21 feet to permit temporary outriggers on the deck of the bridge to transport concrete on standard gauge tramways from a concrete mixing plant on the east side of the river. The tramway operated by motor driven cables three quarters of an inch in diameter, which ran over pulleys and drums at four miles per hour. A tension carriage with counterweights kept the cable line tight.

Two piers located in the forebay were in sixteen feet of water. Excavation work was accomplished using open coffer dams. All other piers were practically on dry ground.

When both ends of the railroad bridge had been completed, it was time to raise the bridge. Using one hundred ton hydraulic jacks operated by high pressure steam pumps, and controlled by a buzzer signal system, the raising began. The bridge raised 32 inches at a time using precast concrete bridge-shoes. At each raising, concrete was poured around these piers. Each, thirty-two inch cycle required eight days to complete.

The raising was carried on progressively from one end of the bridge to the other. Timber shoring transmitted the load of the girders to the jacks. Suspended from the deck girder spans, safety working platforms were built for the men who worked around the piers.

Diversion of rail traffic began December 7, 1925. Each day during the raising, an eight hour construction rest period allowed freight and passenger trains to pass overhead. Then, the cycle steps would be repeated using jacks. The final raising was completed December 15, 1927.

Materials used on this project included 8,000 precast concrete blocks and an additional 6,000 yards of concrete just for these piers. Since the original depot would go under water, a new one had to be constructed, as well.

"The Bureau of Reclamation built a new station in the Spanish style for the Oregon Short Line Railroad at a cost of $30,000. Uncommonly beautiful, it was considered the finest structure of its kind between Pocatello, Idaho, and Portland, Oregon.  The depot

opened to the traveling public March 21, 1926.

# CHAPTER NINE

# BUREAU of RECLAMATION

The Bureau of Reclamation, in 1907, projected the need to move the town, especially the Riverside Addition. It began platting a new townsite on higher ground and making plans to move to higher ground.

The first world war put those plans on hold. However, several years of severe drought conditions kept the idea of a damsite at American Falls alive.

The obstacles were many, including surrounding states who wanted the project to fail. In 1920, the first Federal funds were allocated to do a preliminary study with Harry Dibble and F.A. Banks in charge of the field force.

After exhaustive investigation Mr. Banks selected American Falls as the best site, the place where the river flowed over a ledge of solid rock making excavation costs minimal and without engineering difficulties. An added advantage for this site was the fact, 100,000 years ago, it had been a natural reservoir when Cedar Butte, northwest of Massacre Rocks, erupted spilling lava and completely filling the river channel. This ancient lava dam had created a lake with a shore line of 125 miles and a capacity of 1,700,000 acre feet of water storage. Much as it has today with its concrete dam. In comparison, Palisades has a storage capacity of 40,900.

February 5, 1923, D.W. Davis, Director of Finance for the Bureau of Reclamation sent a telegram verifying that, *"$2,000,000 will be released for the purchase of Right of Way, including Indian Lands, construction work, and railroad contract."* This was believed to be the largest single allotment ever made in the history of the Bureau.

Even though money had been appropriated by Congress, none would be released until all farmers indebtedness had been cleared up. Another requirement was the payment, in advance, of $200,000 by the water districts. This was a stiff requirement indeed since the farmers had not had any crops for several years due to drought.

With the allocation of funds, final decisions on the dam had to be made in Denver. The Bureau of Reclamation Board Engineer Director, Dr. Elwood Mead, recommended a concrete, gravity-type dam be built, from the west riverbank to the high school building. it would be an earth fill dam from that point to the end.

President W. H. Wattis and Superintendent Paddock of Utah Construction Company, and Superintendent Armstrong of the Oregon Short Line Railroad, conferred with Engineer F. A. Banks of the Reclamation Service to review preparatory work such as gravel deposits, work camp location, and side tracks, all of which claimed their full attention.

August 7, 1924, W.G. Swendsen, Commissioner of Reclamation, announced that construction on the dam may being within 30 days, depending upon the weather. Heavy equipment would be made available from the Black Canyon Dam at Emmett, and, additional equipment would come from Yakima, Washington. In such matters, the drawing up plans, arranging finances, and forming working networks move slowly.

The Appraisal Board completed its work. "With respect to the American Falls Project, Indians and settlers, together with the Reclamation Service, and the Congress of the United States apparently settled on a policy." Senator Smoot promised, "… to hurry a Bill through the Senate eliminating provisions and conditions that might prevent the government from participating early on in the plans. Congressman Smith introduced a Bill in the House of Representatives to take care of matters.

Machinery would do much of the work on the dam. both the new railroad bed and the new dam are designed to lie practically parallel to one another. Electric power will probably be used since the largest power plant in Idaho is within a few hundred feet. Instead of using trucks or wagons, materials will be hauled over side tracks.

Everything happening at American Falls caught the attention of the entire nation. The magnitude of the project captured the imagination. Unfortunately, the nationwide news encouraged men to go west. Hundreds were stopped from coming but men by the hundreds continued to come. As increasing numbers continued to arrive, often bringing their families with them, it created a hardship with no local resources to help.

Local newspapers cautioned, "...rumors circulating in far places should not be heeded. There is no employment to warrant such haste at this time. People will do well to make inquiry before they break up homes to come here to find employment. It is next to impossible to find a house for families. Many families are homeless."

"Men are coming in numbers greater than can be employed. The highway between Pocatello and American Falls is populated with pedestrians".

The Utah Construction Company adopted a policy of short term employment in order to provide a meal ticket for as many men as possible, an effort to ease suffering.[18]

By May 1925, slow, steady progress had been made on a small work camp. In a small way, the arrival of one freight car loaded with

---

[18] February 5, 1925 American Falls Chamber of Commerce

lumber and timbers ordered from Coast Mills marked the beginning, of excavation work on the dam. These supplies were used to build coffer dams which allowed men to work below water level to reach bedrock. With seventy-five men on payroll, the Utah Construction added, "The number working will slowly increase."

"The first casualty happened this afternoon at 3:30 March 12th and resulted in the loss of an arm by Roy Renshaw, a fireman on the steam shovel operated by Utah Construction Company. The shovel was engaged in clearing bedrock. For some reason the cable became dead and Renshaw climbed the boom to adjust it and in doing so stepped on the throttle and started the engine. His right arm was caught in the gearing. He was an experienced employee of the company, familiar with what he was doing. The same day, three men working for Utah Construction Company drowned when their boat capsized.[19]

Preliminary stages passed this week when Utah Construction Company began pouring concrete into the first big piers that will separate the water gates in the foundation of the dam. Early in the

---

[19] American Falls Press

week, nine false piers were built on bedrock in the first section of the dam. The nine forms built underneath the trestle work would carry concrete trains out into the dam.

Pouring of concrete into the forms began with only one concrete mixer working. Men working inside the forms tamped the concrete as it came out of the chutes. The false work will be removed to allow the trackage to rest on the concrete. Another concrete mixer will be put into operation when necessity demands.[20]

Working conditions were far from ideal but men were grateful for the chance to have a job. Twelve hour work shifts paid more than a man could expect to be paid for one weeks work otherwise. Once a man landed a job on the dam, he could not afford to miss a day for any reason. If he was late at the beginning of a shift or missed a day, his position would be given to the next man in line. Even a family funeral was not excused. It didn't matter, his job was gone. When he returned, he had to get back in line with all of the other hopefuls.

---

[20] source unidentified.

Many local men were employed on the construction sites. Walter Bethke explained, "It was most exciting. There were three crews of 300 men each. One crew was working, one crew was sleeping and one crew was drinking. American Falls was a rough town then, offering many ways to lose your hard earned money. The men worked for $3.60 a day and were thankful for it. If any crew member missed a day, they were out of work."

Edward Rast agreed, "If a feller got sick, somebody would take his job; then when he got better he had to stand in line again along with all the others wanting a job, and there would be a hundred at least in that line!

"I liked working there, it was so interesting to watch how the equipment worked. There were so many machines, everything was new to me.

"I especially liked to watch the big mule teams pulling the Fresal Scraper. And, them mules was smart, too. They could tell time! When the noon whistle blew, they quit and would not budge until they got unhitched. They wanted a rest just like the men. Not until the whistle blew again would they go back to work! I never did get along good with mules but I had to admire how smart those animal really are and strong, too. Big teams of twenty and forty mules worked on the dam. It was something to see."[21]

Work continued until final completion when slowly, water began to rise behind the new dam. The former sidewalks and tree lined streets slipped under water. Only the tree tops gave proof that a thriving community of theaters, businesses, hotels, railroad and hospital had once been there. Rows of dying tree tops left a visible, sad reminder for many years.

"No longer are there magnificent halls for entertainment and recreation. No vigorous dancing on Saturday night. No wonderful, lavish Remington Hotel to receive guests by sending carriages to meet all six daily passenger trains.

"On the other hand, there are no cowboys causing rampage in town. The old water wagon is outdated and gone. Gone too is the old hitching rack near the mortuary."[22]

---

[21] personal oral histories — Ella Rast

[22] Bertha Sawyer The Idaho State Journal

January 17, 1927, Idaho Power issued a curious reminder: *'The Idaho Power Company conveyed Title of their land to the United States government several years ago. The dam structure is all in place and the company is busy stopping leaks. Owners of livestock grazing on reservoir Right of Way, must remove their animals to protect themselves against loss, as of January 20th. Water levels are soon expected to rise five feet.'*

What an odd announcement considering all the publicity throughout the entire nation over the past four years. Perhaps some did not believe the water could reach twenty five miles up river. Whatever the reason, many settlers did lose livestock in the rising waters.

Meanwhile, for years, the public had questioned the soundness of the wooden bridge crossing the Snake River at American Falls. Merchants in American Falls denied the charges the old bridge to be unsafe for fear of losing westside business. Aberdeen merchants were angry and afraid to transport their supplies across the swaying bridge. They accused the local merchants of trying to put them out of business by making them travel through Blackfoot to reach the railroad. The arguments were heated and everyone had an opinion.

The state and County officials denied a problem existed with the wooden wagon bridge structure as it stood. West side travelers were not in agreement and began to demand improved public road conditions for travel convenience. Rumors persisted that the structure was unsafe.

During construction of the dam, public pressure became insistent that something must be done to replace it and that work on the new vehicle bridge must take priority.

At last, the United States Government posted guards at either end to keep people off the shaky bridge. July of 1927, part of the bridge piers washed away! Fortunately, no one was on the bridge at the time.

With the wagon bridge gone and the dam construction completed, the government made modifications and began to build a new roadway on top of the new dam at a cost on $100,000. With this roadway, the quarrel between American Falls and Aberdeen quickly faded.

Today, the significance of this concrete structure is not appreciated for what it truly represents. Gigantic structures quickly dwarfed this forerunner that struggled and fought for its very birth right. Despite the small size in caparison to the giants arriving later, few dams around the world can boast of the same amazing agricultural and economic impact. The irrigation system it fostered resulted in new communities, new schools, and new opportunities.

Few dams, can boast of being profitable as quickly as this one. Bringing water to the most fertile soil in the world has had a far reaching affect. The economic impact is huge. Without water, southeastern Idaho is an arid desert, where crops shrivel. With water, the positive impact is felt all the way to Washington D. C. and would be sorely missed nationwide.

This small concrete dam is probably the only one that paid for itself in the first few years. It is the only one which struggling farmers themselves were required to pay one third of the construction costs in advance, before any work began. Every one should be familiar with this historical dam. It is a concrete example of what 'people power' can accomplish. Success on this very spot changed agricultural possibilities and Idaho Power changed how individuals work and live.

# CHAPTER TEN

# STRUGGLE to FUND ONE DAM

A multitude of irrigation companies sprang up, some merged, some failed. The Aberdeen-Springfield Canal company is still in business.

A community of Mexican families had settled in the Rock Creek Valley. After successfully irrigating since 1877, Guadelupe Valdez obtained the <u>first irrigation rights</u> on February 15, 1879. However, severe harassment by the cattlemen caused most of them to return south.

Probably the first irrigation efforts took place near 'The Bottoms', at Michaud Flats, in 1860. Rockland, also, had a small successful irrigation system in 1879. Under direction of Western Water Company promoters from Chicago, Mr. Duke Fargo and Mr. Harvey, the first big irrigation project near American Falls began, in 1882.

The landowners of Warm Creek and Neeley formed an irrigation cooperative and provided the hand labor for building the dam using a

Fresal scraper and animal teams at Indian Springs. A small canal ran ten mile north toward Michaud.

Unfortunately, the water behind this dam formed a 40 acre lake only a few inches deep. The project was abandoned after the second washout, in 1890. Today, Rockland Road runs across the top of that early dam.

Around 1900, at the 4500 foot elevation, the precipitation had been reported to be above average and to fall at an advantageous time with cool nights making successful dry land farming possible.

Agriculture dreams became more exciting after Senator Carey of Wyoming secured the CAREY LAND ACT, in 1894. Each western state was empowered to sell water right to 1,000,000 acres of land. The state sold this land for fifty cents an acre.

By 1902, the hundreds of working engineers led to the formation of the Bureau of Reclamation Service. With fertile soil, sunshine and irrigation water, a farmer can be the master of his own destiny and enjoy farming as a safer and profitable investment.

Based upon the estimated cost of construction and 6% interest, the water rights were originally set at $25.00 per acre. Defaulted contracts were reclaimed as Carey Land. This Act rivaled the Homestead Act in importance because it assured water storage facilities for millions of acres.

In 1882, Congress sent I. B. Perrine, an engineer, to southeast Idaho to do a feasibility study for a dam at American Falls. He determined it was not only feasible but essential for agriculture to assure adequate storage of water in drought years. Such a dam had the advantage of being located where there had once been an ancient reservoir with a large capacity.

For fifty years, he fought for the dam and met with strong resistance. His own Blue Lakes farm, with its fertile soil and irrigation, proved an abundance of fresh fruits and vegetables could be produced. The demand for fresh produce being high, he shipped to Twin Falls, to Albion Normal School and to Ketchum miners.

The resistance against a dam at American Falls had continued, since 1882, despite the proven economic benefits shown by small dams. However, the negative impact of the First World War, immediately was followed by a devastating Post War Depression. Both were a severe blow to every business. In Idaho, the situation was compounded by an unprecedented prolonged drought. The disaster placed the state of Idaho at risk of ruin.

Governor Davis recognized that unless aggressive action were taken financial collapse for his state was inevitable. Crop feature due to drought meant farmers could not repay loans. That left banks unable to meet their obligations crumbling like autumn leaves. The state revenues were dismal. It seemed hopeless.

The one bright hope on the horizon remained the securing of water. The Governor strongly believed a dam at American Falls would bring happy times to the state. A large dam would remove a major risk from farming. Since funding for this dam had withdrawn several times already, the pressure was on and the story moves like a mystery, with adventure, tension, and intrigue.

To find a way to build the dam, he appointed Irvin E. Rockwell of the State Board of Education with proven negotiation and organizational skills to achieve that goal.[23]

As it happens, they learned that the new Secretary of Interior, Mr. Albert Fall of New Mexico, an oil tycoon, has no connection with or sympathy for irrigation projects. He was invited to Idaho for an inspection of the potential project, in October 1920. Hot and dusty travel conditions over long distances and on unimproved roads proved unpleasant. He was cross but noncommittal.

Mr. Fall did meet with the power company officials who were given an understanding that before the dam could be constructed the power company would have to relocate the power plant. Mr. Fall agreed to compensate the firm for relocation costs of building the new plant. However, Mr. Fall did not sign this contract between the power company and the government at the time of his visit, in October. It had a deadline of January 13th.

Afterwards, apparently the notion of rebuilding a town, moving a railroad, building a power plant and constructing a dam were

---

[23] Saga of the American Falls Dam Irvin Rockwell

excessive expenditures. He especially disapproved of the current delinquencies and severe drought problems of farmers in the Twin Falls area were of no concern to him. Mr. Fall changed his mind. "— I don't like it a damn," he said. "...let them stew in their own juice."

Meanwhile, the power company unaware of his change of mind, began construction.

When the people in Boise learned of the missing signature, concern began to mount. Then they learned, Mr. Fall had slipped out of the country; he could not be found for discussion by any means! He had vanished. The political drama began to worsen.

In December of 1921, Mr. Rockwell had been reluctantly drawn into working with the Irrigation District and met briefly with Barry Dibble (Minidoka) in American Falls. As the meeting began, an unbelieving Rockwell heard the announcement that the American Falls project had been abandoned! Stunned! Rockwell knew the dreams of an Idaho agricultural empire rested on the completion of this project! The fast approaching agreement deadline expired January 13th, 1922.

News of this announcement would cause panic in Idaho. An emergency meeting to discuss strategies was held in Boise with, among others, Frank A. Banks (Jackson Lake Dam), Frank E. Weymouth (Arrowrock Dam), Ben Stoutemyer (legal counsel).

What could be done? It seemed hopeless until Rockwell pointed out two things. -1- The government was obligated to pay Idaho Power Company whether the dam was built or not. -2- If all the irrigation districts consolidated, their combined numbers would represent a strong force. The major negative was the outstanding loan payments on the Minidoka project, of $560,000.

Valiantly fighting to save the project, Mr. Rockwell and Senator Borah went to Washington D.C. and on the strength of the power company claim, at the eleventh hour, managed to obtain a Court Order signed by Judge Arthur Davis, allowing an extension until June.

The audacious, Mr. Fall did not return until February 13th, more than thirty days later. Senator Borah was waiting. Mr. Fall commented to Senator Borah, "You resurrected a Corpse!"

Senator Borah continued to work with Mr. Fall until he conceded to go forward but "only if all arrears in the amount of $560,000 had been paid up by farmers". Mr. Fall had no sympathy with the extenuating circumstances of depression or severe drought. But without water there could be no crops with which the farmers could acquire money.

The governor had hoped to get a reversal of the delinquencies. Instead, all he got from Mr. Fall was his demand of a down payment on the new dam in advance.

Undaunted, Governor Davis, the dynamic spark plug for the irrigation movement, used his influence with Mr. Fall hoping to reverse his disastrous decision. The projected financial benefits far exceeded the cost of the project. He had presented Fall with the facts relating to the positive influence water would have on southeastern Idaho. On the other hand, one severe drought in 1919 caused a twenty-five million dollar loss in crops, a loss greater than the cost of the $ 5,800,000. cost of the entire project.[24]

---

[24] 'Saga of the American Falls Dam Irvin Rockwell

In non drought years, crops had grown in abundance under limited irrigation in recent years. The agricultural product had filled 6,700 freight cars and created 22,008 farms! In just ten years, new towns were growing where there had been nothing. The potential benefits of this irrigation project justified the 60,000 acre sacrifice of choice land going under water.

The governor argued that the extreme financial hardship of the farmers was not their fault but the result of postwar depression and the drought. Inflexible to the end, Mr. Fall required full payment of unpaid farmer debts.

Meanwhile, in Boise, the governor, set up a rescue program as the team continued to work out a strategy before the June deadline. Abandonment of the project seemed certain. Rockwell asked Warren G. Swenden, State Commissioner of Reclamation, to direct his intelligence toward finding a solution.

Warren Swendsen pointed out since the government was already obligated to the power company for a large sum, perhaps there was a chance. The people of south east Idaho had to be informed about the pending catastrophe. An immediate, intensive campaign was undertaken. If money were not raised immediately, everyone would lose. At great personal expense good people worked long days to overcome fears, objections, and to focus on the outcome.

Rockwell worked exclusively with Major Reed, Henry McCormick and Ben E. Stoutemyer who sold his brainchild of consolidating al the irrigation districts to Governor Davis. An impossible concept but at this time of "great emergency", it worked. Once the irrigation districts united, they were serious force.

The news media picked up the story nationwide with sensational news coverage. Support poured in from Idaho and from around the nation. In less than two weeks sufficient money had been raised to prepare a new document allowing dam construction to proceed. Secretary of Interior, Mr. Fall, still refused to sign so, on June 27, 1922, the document was signed by assistant Secretary, E.D. Finney.

The governor expressed his appreciation "—to the thousands of participants in the great enterprise, including important personnel of the government, — so that all obstructions — had been — outwitted on their own ground."

With many of the uncertainties of the past fourteen years cleared away, American Falls could finally enter into an new era of public spiritedness. The little city became the most advertised community in the nation with features appearing in all the major newspapers.

At last, January 15th, 1923, an Election would be held giving all residents in the county an opportunity to vote for or against the new dam. The day was declared a holiday. To help defray expenses, the City Council received a two hundred dollar anonymous donation. Free train rides and over 70 automobiles were used to carry voters to the polls.[25]

"The little agricultural hamlet of American Falls, Idaho, has consented to move to a new site to make way for the construction of the largest reservoir in the country — a $12,000,000 project with a capacity of 1,500,000 acre feet of water. Before long the present site of the town will be inundated under millions of gallons of water."

New York Herald

---

[25] American Falls Press

# CHAPTER ELEVEN

# CORNERSTONE CELEBRATION

Nearly fifty years years of controversy had surrounded building a dam at American Falls because the town site would be flooded and because valuable land would be lost forever. Valid reasons. The opinions were strongly divided, and, everyone had an opinion.

At last, it appeared the dam would be built. Preliminary preparations began with the government purchasing all land that would be flooded which included the town and 'The Bottoms'. The government would develop a new townsite with water, sewer and streets.

Eighteen months after the Vote approving the dam, the mood was ripe for a celebration. Construction on the dam had begun in February. Unprecedented enthusiasm for the American Falls Dam Celebration had spread throughout the nation. It was the topic of conversation in Idaho and communities in Idaho as far away as Weiser organized caravans of automobiles to attend the celebration.

Minidoka County planned to send a monster caravan of 500 cars. Gooding and Shoshone also sent a huge caravan. Someone said, "There will be no one left in Boise except the janitor."

The state planning committee scheduled the event to begin at 8 am on Monday, July 13, 1925. This event meant more to the state than a mere holiday! It was a victory celebration! To make it an unqualified success, nothing must be overlooked. Thousands of people began arriving before Saturday.

The new city was in a rough, primitive, incomplete state of development. Most of the old town structures had been moved leaving the ground broken down into a fine dusty powder two feet deep. Accommodations for a crowd of twenty thousand people had not been anticipated. Hotels were not necessarily ready for visitors. Little is documented about the hot and dusty conditions. Apparently the crowd focused on the grand scope and magnitude of the celebration activities.

The official opening to lay the cornerstone was scheduled for Monday morning. Unofficially, at one minute past midnight Sunday night, the people opened the activities with a street dance that continued until dawn. It was one gigantic party in the streets.

According to Pearl Watts, "The big crowd made it the awfulest mess you ever saw, just all kinds of people. There were construction workers, hobos, curious onlookers and politicians. And the dust was two feet deep from moving all the buildings. Mostly, everybody drank and many got drunk. People slept in the street or stayed all night in the pool halls. I was afraid of the crowd and spent the night at the Depot where my husband worked the night shift."

"A exciting day to remember with real entertainment from far away." Edward Rast recalled, "A day of celebration and history. Entertainment was in the air as well as on the ground. I seen the air show from where I was working on the dam. Airplanes doing tricks, and parachute jumps, and even women standing out on the wings. All kinds of foolishness. During the day one shift of construction workers mingled at the ceremonies, and then they went to work to make way for the night crew of five hundred men to come."

On July 13, 1925, the historic ceremony to lay the cornerstone for the new dam took place in what then remained of the original town. It was a day of confusion, speeches and entertainment.

Presiding over the ceremonies as master of ceremonies, was Mr. R.E. Shepherd, and Judge O.R. Baum, of Pocatello, chairman for the state committee in charge. Other dignitaries present included: W.F. Howard and Guy Flemmer of the Reclamation Association; A.C. Milner and Clarence Milner of Milner Dam; Joel L. Priest of the Oregon Short Line Railroad; Secretary of Interior Hubert Work; Commissioner of Reclamation Elwood Mead; Irwin Rockwell Public Relations for the State; U.S. Senator William E. Borah; Idaho Governor Charles C. Moore; Utah Governor George Dern; Congressman Smith and Congressman Burton L. Fremont; and of the Bannock Indian Tribes.

The program opened with an aerial bombardment of fireworks, various types of sputter bombs, parachutes, smoke rockets and other things to attract the eyes upward to enjoy an exciting aerial show. The occasion of laying the cornerstone prompted many patriotic speeches under the hot sun to a patient audience standing without the benefit of shade or grass. Context of the speeches included a review of the struggles preceding this big day.

O. A. Fitzgerald of the Salt Lake Tribune documented his observations of the historic occasion. "Two generations of empire builders came into their own on that day. A silent immovable barrier of concrete, rock, and steel creating a lake of 1,700,000 acres of water needed to nourish crops stretching for hundreds of miles. Today, a spectacular project has begun which will prove it self in history and gem state visionaries who labored for twenty five years to see this day, will live to se the fruits of their labors. The people are deserving of at least one day to discharge enthusiasm.

"Today American Falls is like a carnival town with crowds shifting about, one moment jovial, the next solemn, involving government officials, state officials, businessmen, public leaders, farmers and visitors all mingled together. It is not a day of hilarity. Businessmen closed their stores, citizens left their homes, farmers dropped their tools for this one day. Construction work continued without interruption. It was the farmers who made the dam a necessity and they supplied the $2,700,000 necessary in order to obtain government aid for the project.

"As is true of many big ventures, they begin with an idea, a vision.  As far as is known, I. B. Perrine, of Idaho Reclamation Bureau, was the first to have this vision, in 1882.  The second generation came with greater capacity for development of the west and the equipment to build a tangible structure assuring ample water to fill ditches when hills are parched from drought and grass is shriveled.

"As the cornerstone slipped into place, sealed by Secretary Work, he reflected on the many times the American Falls Dam had been doomed, heartbreaking moments."[26]

Commissioner Elwood Mead spoke briefly to explain, "The building of the American Falls Dam is the most successful and most significant instance of cooperation between the people of our state and the government.  The confidence shown by the people of this locality is one of the greatest achievements in the Reclamation Bureau

---

[26] Salt Lake Tribune by O. A. Fitzgerald July 1925

and one of the reasons we have confidence in its future. We meet here in a pleasant frame of mind."

A reading of **President Calvin Coolidge's** Telegram acknowledging the occasion, follows:

"The meeting to celebrate the beginning of the construction of storage works at American Falls has for me unusual interest because there is included... an element of self-help indicated by the settlers with the payment in advance of a large part of the construction cost.

"No clearer evidence could be furnished of the value of irrigation and the confidence in its agricultural future than has been shown by their contributions and cooperation toward this undertaking. Please convey my congratulations on the Occasion.

With great dignity and sadness, the most poignant speech was presented by a member of the Bannock Indian tribe, clothed in the colorful regalia and huge feathered bonnet of a chief.

In measured stately stride, Chief Tea Pokribo was ushered onto the platform to address the multitude. He turned his gaze to Secretary Work and without any formality began to speak. His speech was given in the Bannock tongue. When translated, it proved a stirring example of the simple, but lofty eloquence of the Indian inspired by an uncommon occasion.

"I consider it a great honor to be permitted to say a few words in behalf of my people on this unusual occasion. I would that I might reach your understanding so that you could realize the very great sacrifice we have made in order that this big dam might blossom into reality.

"I was one of the delegates who went to Washington in behalf of my people and agreed to the flooding of our lands. In giving up forever this large tract of our land necessary for your great reservoir we are sharing with you our limited supply of bread. We needed this land to supply our humble needs. No one, not a member of our tribe, can understand what this sacrifice means to us. It was a good part of our inheritance. It is a part of our winter home.

"Our life is simple based on the land. We give it up because this reservoir will provide homes for many white people. It is only because of this that we have consented to share our lands with you. We realize that you are great and strong. We are poor, humble and few in number. You are growing more powerful, we are growing weaker.

"In talks with our reservation superintendent we saw what this great work means to your government. We felt it was our duty to make the sacrifice. The water stored here will make homes for multitudes of white people. And more than all, we want to live in peace and harmony with our white brother. We want you to be our good friend. We want to improve our homes and farms on land that is left. We want our children to grow up to be good men and women, just like your children grow up to be good men and women.

"We have no other flag. We know only our common country which this flag represents. (Saluting and pointing to the American flag.)

"We only ask that you be patient with us. Bear with us and help us in our humble simple ways. Help us to educate our children and to care for our sick ones. Help us to learn continuing obedience and respect for your laws.

"We want to be a part of this great nation that controls all of this country which once was ours. We are trying to adapt our ways to your ways. With your continued consideration and fair treatment we shall succeed."[27]

Hundreds of Indians came to join in and provided a huge barbecue feast of several beef. For them this was a day of mourning. The Indians grieved bitterly over the loss of their precious 'Bottom Lands' as each day they moved their tents a little further back and still further from the encroaching waters.

Following Chief Tea Pokribo's address, an exceptional, original historical pageant was presented; one which rivaled the laying of the cornerstone in significance. Presented in tableau, the pageant

---

[27] Saga of the American Falls Dam by IE Rockwell

embodied eight episodes, designated as Lewis and Clark, Fur Trading,

Pony Express, Covered Wagons, Fort Bridger Treaty, Indian School,

Mormon Migration and Our Present Day. Included as a part of

the pageant was a monster parade of floats and marching groups from

various institutions and communities interested in the American Falls

development.

Unfortunately, no known copy of the manuscript is available

today.

A word about Irvin E. Rockwell, without whom, the project may

never have reached completion. This man had never really been

involved in irrigation; he was an educator with the State Education

Department. But, when asked to step forward he did so with rare

diplomacy and revived the project when it seemed doomed. When

construction began, modestly, he said, 'I have kept myself submerged

in multiple activities working for the completion of this great project,

since late 1921. Now that it is over, that is glory enough.'

His efforts are widely appreciated because he grasped the

significance of unity. Without the consolidation of all irrigation districts, the project would have died. He was aware and disturbed with knowledge that interests outside Idaho had already applied for specific water rights and were working against our dam should the American Falls project fail. He understood that present water rights within our state had to be retained. Had the dam failed, Idaho Power Company would have lost its right to water as well.

Rockwell said, "The success of the American Falls project is an outstanding example of cooperation and unselfish service, of staying on the job through good and evil reports, thick with hostility and often violent opposition from high places that finally triumphed in fine style.'"[28]

---

[28] SAGA of the American Falls Dam by I. Rockwell

# CHAPTER TWELVE

# THE DRAMA OF MOVING A TOWN

Few cities hold the distinction claimed by American Falls, Idaho. The first time an entire town had been moved, one mile, to higher ground. This happened within eighteen months, between 1923 and 1925! Never had such an expensive event been recorded. It became the topic of conversation all over the nation. Newspapers across the country followed the details with interviews, feature stories and pictures.

To grasp the scope of the project, imagine a freight train three and a half miles long. The train stops at American Falls and unloads a cargo of gravel, cement, lumber and reinforcing steel, the amount of materials required to construct only the new million dollar Idaho Power Company power plant.[29]

A small part of the three projects.

---

[29] Legacy of Light' by Stacy smith

Plans for the new townsite, consisting of 300 acres, had been drawn up by Russell V. Black, an expert city planner. He platted the 300 acres into 867 lots. His plan called for a seven acre Town Square which he envisioned would be surrounded by the court house, city hall, library, apartment houses, and churches. The park would be beautified with shrubs and trees and maintained for two years. The new town was free of bonded indebtedness of any kind. Total cost to improve the town site was $400,000. with an additional $10,000 set aside for beautification.

Snippets from the newspaper reported that the 'Bird Findlayson and his crew poured concrete for the new court house early in the week and are far along in completing their contract.'

'In January, Ernest White and Company encountered a lot of rock at the new $80,000 high school. Construction work has not been materially delayed. The forms are now all in and most of the concrete has been poured into the foundation.'

Local officials found themselves in the heart of the unfolding drama and met frequently to make important decisions for the new community. In October 1923, Mr. F.A. Banks met with the city council at the Court House and reported, "Approximately $65,000 will be available for building sidewalks and curbing in the new town. The City Council authorized the Reclamation Service to install concrete culverts and cement drains at an actual cost of approximately $7000.00.

In the spring of 1924, 'construction work began on a new Boise-Payette Lumber yard. The American Falls Mills and the Zaring Grain Company relocated at considerable expense and loss of time but despite the inconvenience, were reaping the reward of enterprise and energy.'

'The trench Digger of the Kennedy Construction Company has encountered problems with cave-ins in February 1924. The sewer pipe trenches are 17 -20 feet deep and are being placed in all of the alleys. The sewers in the new model city are sufficiently deep to drain every basement according to engineer Banks. Good progress has been made but a vast amount of work remains.'

'Alworth and Sayer announced, "Pipes for the new water system have been contracted and are expected to arrive soon. Construction will begin soon and once the pipes are in place, the graveling of the new streets can go forward.' "Considerable savings were made on the sewer system. Council members were assured that, "In no case has the actual contract price been exceeded from the original estimate."

'Streets were graded and surfaced with gravel on the lower end of the Oregon Trail Street, on March 27, 1924. Large areas are set aside for parks and schools.'

'The City Council approved the purchase of pumps and equipment. Options under consideration for transporting water from the west side of the river to the new east side city reservoir included:

-1- Fluming the water across the river on piers.

-2- Fluming under the water on the river bed.

-3- Piping water across on the dam itself.

The latter was chosen as being the cheapest and the best in the long run.[30]

---

[30] October 25, 1923: American Falls Press

'With construction on the 1,500,000 gallon city reservoir completed, the reservoir could receive water from the Tucker (Reuger) Spring on the west side. By the end of July 1924, residents anywhere in the new city would have fresh water on tap.'

'Ben Sills of the Reclamation Service, announced, "Two miles of sidewalk have been laid. Six more miles will be completed in the next few months by a crew of forty men. The work is proceeding at the rate of 700 feet per day. Regarding employment. Men approach me daily, seeking employment. I have worked for many years in construction in every state in the Union but have never seen labor so plentiful."[31]

Local newspapers gave glowing commendation upon the completion of white accented brick Power County Court House. Insisting, 'it was the most conspicuous accomplishment this far. The building promises a bright future for the new community."[32]

---

[31] October 25, 1923: American Falls Press

[32] December 1925 American Falls Press

As the deadline to move out of the original town site neared, the population lacked signs of enthusiastic endorsement in accepting the new townsite. Questions asked included, "Of all the ground around between here and Pocatello, is this the very best place to build a new town? Except for speculators, opinions were generally negative.

At first the townspeople had been quite pleased to have a large dam built near their town. Now, the idea of moving did not appeal to them at all. They didn't think much of it.

Even though inevitable, acceptance was slow.

Finally, to show support for the project, a few prominent families began building new homes in the 'Reclamation Addition'. Encouraged, a few families began to purchase lots. One early report, in 1923, declared that twenty new foundations had been completed and after seasoning, would be ready to receive a home in May of 1924.

With minimum investment in equipment, entrepreneurs began to dig basements and pour new foundations. Gradually, a new town sprouted on the higher ground above the river where there had been nothing a few months earlier.

During the week of March 12th, 1925, the citizens with the distinction of being the first to move are the following: J.A Edwards, W.M. Davis (brick home), F.H. Hook, Arthur Davis, and A.J. Twoomey (Dome house).33 Still, citizens were slow to take action.

June 11, 1925, Mr. F. A. Banks spoke at Chamber of Commerce pointing out that one third of the allotted time had elapsed and only one sixth of the houses have been moved. "If residents do not contract to move soon, they will be paying higher prices to move."[34]

Three hundred and fifty buildings moved one mile, an event without precedent. First, the Federal Reclamation Service would purchase all property affected by rising water.

This historic event, occurred during an economically tough time following WORLD WAR I and several sever drought years. Although the government had been more than fair with property offers, many families still did not have enough money to do what was necessary in order to make the move to higher ground. Each piece of

---

[33] March 12, 1925 American Falls Press

[34] American Falls Press

property, no matter how small, had to be repurchased separately and moved.

If property owners held out or refused to sell to the government, their property was condemned and then given a fair appraisal; the owner still had to leave his place. He could not stay where flood waters were certain to come.

After the government had purchased all affected properties, every property was offered for sale as salvage. The former owner was given the first right of refusal. People could purchase their former home or any different building. Keeping the cost low enough was done to encourage sales and at the same time, rapidly remove the government from the house moving business. It was intended homeowners should be able to reestablish on the new site with money left to put it back into original shape.

'The government also announced a bargain sale on all buildings that could not be moved from the old town site. These were sold for salvage purposes only.[35]

---

[35] Feb. 26. 1926 American Falls Press

Concerned about the failure of homeowners to make contract arrangements to move, an organization formed to assist homeowners with moving expenses by loaning money for that purpose and to speed up the moving to the Reclamation Addition. Payment to be made on a monthly basis. With this assistance, moving should become active earlier than had seemed possible.

According to Tom Sparks, "An owner had three choices. He could move his own building and be reimbursed by the government. Or the government would buy and move the building after which the owner could buy it back. The owner could sell his building to another person making them responsible for the expense of moving.

"It didn't matter a lot which method you chose, you lost financially. You had to pay for a new basement and the new foundation. You had to build new steps and porches, and purchase new shrubs and lawn. The government did not reimburse your total costs.

"The entire moving process did test the old pioneer spirit of American Falls citizens to make the Magic Valley what it is today."[36]

Snows and rains had kept the ground soft but soon the weather would improve. Confidently, the Reclamation Service pointed out to the reluctant, "Dwellings will be at a premium when dam construction begins and happy will be the family who has a home of its own and at a figure that offers a fine opportunity for profit on the investment. As a whole, it appears that American Falls people are going to be well satisfied with the results of the move."

During the year 1925, men were working feverishly to assemble equipment capable of moving all of the buildings. At that time there were two blacksmith shops in operation, Clem Abercrombie and Bob King. They practically worked day and night to transform abandoned threshing machines and ancient steam engines salvaged from deserted mining camps and lumber camps.

It was an innovative assortment of trucks and rusty wheels and any parts that could be transformed into a working machine. Wheels

---

[36] personal source... Nancy Sparks Laurence

were reinforced with modern bellies. Some of these contrivances collapsed under the weight of their burden.

The government moved a few test houses to establish an average cost per building.[37]

Among the house movers, a few were experienced and well equipped. Frank Mitchell, John Larson and Porter. John Larson had designed modern equipment capable of moving 150,000 pounds. Under their supervision, trucks built to specification could turn in a very small radius with engine capable of most any task.

Larsen had been a resident of Rockland fourteen years earlier. He had moved to Iowa to learn the moving trade and returned ready to participate in the house moving business at hand. In March 1925, he said, "We are ready to go as soon as the ground is firmer."

In most instances, trucks hauled everything movable to the new site. The larger structures required larger equipment and greater ingenuity. it was claimed that moves were accomplished without

---

[37] June 11, 1925 American Falls Press

damaging plaster walls. However, a wall and ceiling repair service was apparently kept busy.

'After it had been determined that a dam would be built putting the town site under water, plans got underway rapidly. The sole agent to handle the sale of lots was the city; lots went on sale October 4, 1923. Businessmen were allowed to determine where they wanted to locate.

At the February 26, 1926 meeting, Mr. M. Meyers, president of Chamber of Commerce said, "Ten months ago there was not a building in the new Reclamation Addition of American Falls. Today we have the appearance of a new city with a full fledged County seat. We have a wonderful water system, new sewers, improved streets, adequate lighting and miles of sidewalks."

'Fifty stores and 300 residences have moved since April 1925. Growth is good. Ten thousand dollars was set aside for trees and parks.'


"The home of J.O. Hiatt is moving today, June 11, 1925. The home of W.L. Newton is being loaded, and, it will be sitting on its new foundation this coming week. The next homes to move are: T.C. Sparks [Lot 9, blk. 47], Dr Logan [Lot 17, blk. 18], H.C. Beatty, S.H. McCullough, Dr Schiltz, E.E. Zaring, O. F. Crowley, J.A. Edwards [Lot 17-18, blk. 24], Charles Stitt [Lot 19, blk. 24], M.A. Workman [Lot 9, blk. 48]. Foundations are already completed."[38]

Nationwide, newspapers followed the drama at American Falls. Perhaps to make it more fun, some people competed testing the extremes as these examples prove. While underway some ladies did not interrupt their bridge games. And, according to rumor, Grace Barnard and Rene Evans were part of one such bridge foursome.

In one instance, since moving day was also baking day, the fire was not put out in the kitchen range. The lady of the house baked her bread while the house moved to its new location.

The moving of St. John's Lutheran Church was delayed to *'Remember the Sabbath Day and keep it Holy.'* Even though

---

[38] June 11, 1925 American Falls Press

mounted on wheels, Reverend Ernest H. Haacke saw no reason why Worship Services should not be conducted as usual. The congregation climbed in using ladders to observe an elevated Worship Service.

With each move, much was learned and many challenges overcome. If one approach did not work, another would be tried. Often equipment being used was crushed under the load. In most instances the problems were solved to the amazement of all.

The Grand Hotel and four grain elevators proved challenging. By the time they got around to these large structures, 350 buildings had been moved.

Moving the three story Grand Hotel proved to be the most difficult. The first attempt moved the building only three blocks. The second attempt got the building within one block of its final destination, when they quit. That left the courageous owners to find a way to drag the building into place using block, tackle, and capstans. Somehow it happened.

The original building had been covered in sheet metal but at the new location, it was refaced in a handsome red brick exterior. Today, the building can be seen on the corner of Tyhee and Roosevelt.

The Oneida elevator, received no Bids. The foundation extended too far into the ground to make it feasible to attempt a move. If dynamited, and at considerable expense, no salvage value would remain. So after removing the wooden structures attached to it, the concrete tower remained standing.

It still stands there today as a silent sentinel over a drowned town, a local landmark, circa 1927.

# CHAPTER THIRTEEN

# DEDICATION of the DAM

Finally, in September 1927, it was time to reflect on all that had taken place. Provided by the federal government, complete with parks, street lighting, graveled streets, water and sewer, the new town was now a reality. What had been unoccupied ground two years ago is now the new city of American Falls. Moving the town from its original location on the east bank of the Snake River had proved a tremendous task, but was accomplished in a short space of time, — less than two years.

A roadway was built on top of the dam at a cost of $100,000, to replace the wooden bridge whose piers had collapsed. This new roadway, known as the Roosevelt Highway, and later, the Transcontinental U.S. Highway 30. To have a dependable, solid way to cross the river pleased the public who had been pleading for a safe bridge for ten years.

"The new Idaho Power Company plant addition at American Falls nearly doubled the capacity making this hydroelectric plant the largest and most important in the Northwest. Not including transmission lines, the total investment of this Public Utility Company exceeds $3,000,000.

"With five generating units running full time, the Plant has a rated capacity of 27,000 kilowatts or 36,000 horse power."[39, 40]

September 28, 1927, the formal dedication honoring the men of vision and dedication that had made it possible, was held.

No one person claims the idea but the credit ought to go to Bert Perrine who fought for the dam for fifty years, since 1892. Congress had sent him to investigate the feasibility of a dam at this site. Despite publicity by Guy Flemmer, and promotional efforts by R. E. Shepherd and Major Reed the project had met with resistance.[41]

Completion of the dam transformed the desert into green gold. This feat happened because a few dedicated leaders fought against insurmountable obstacles over many years to finally secure a reliable

---

[39] September 22, 1927 American Falls Press

[40] In 1977 the plant was upgraded to produce 100,000 kilowatts. It is capable of 57.5 megawatts.

[41] American Falls Press

source of water and remove the fear of drought. Impounding upper

Snake River waters in the reservoir represents a mighty achievement.

# CHAPTER FOURTEEN

# The EYE WITNESSES STORIES

# TOM DILLIE—REMEMBERS

"It wasn't until the spring of 1926 that Mr. Porter Mitchell was badly in need of help with raising the old Standard Grain Elevator. In order to raise this enormous building high enough to put timbers and trucks under it, it was determined we had to use at least sixteen men. Each man was to attend one screw jack and turn it a quarter turn, then crib it up with heavy blocking. When finished, the men moved to the other side where the same thing would be done. The cribbing was a slow, careful operation requiring frequent checks.

"Heavy timbers long enough to reach under the entire building were placed on the trucks. But, before trucks could be wheeled underneath, the building had to be raised five feet. But, before any weight of the building touched the trucks, first a pit had to be dug underneath the building deep enough to allow to move underneath and be level. Next a driveway of compacted dirt was built coming out of the pit which kept the trucks level.

"After getting our enormous Standard Grain Elevator building loaded on the trucks, next came the problem of moving it using steam engines belonging to Ben Cotant, Nash Quad Truck, and White Truck. The Nash Quad was a four wheel drive government truck used in WWI. Its tires were hard rubber and only four inches wide and could not get traction in the loose sand.

Back in those days, paved streets were unknown. In fact, not many streets even had a layer of gravel. Moving buildings into new town, crossed the railroad tracks at the eastern end of the dam where the Oregon Trail turns near the old Washington School; at this point, a difficult sandy spot was a challenge for the heavy equipment. To give assistance to the massive motorized equipment, an enormous span of black draft horses stood ready.

"The sprinkler wagon was kept in constant use because the heavy equipment created a dust bowl. The sprinkler wagon made frequent trips to the fire hydrant. It was used to harden the ground as well but water could not help at this sandy spot.

"The huge buildings needed all the assistance we could draft to get our burden up the hill into the new town. Three elevators, the Evan, The Standard, and the Globe Mills, were moved in the same way. The old Standard eventually burned and was replaced by the Power County Grain Growers modern cement bins.

"The one grain elevator that did not get moved was cement structure which can be seen standing in the water today. It was determined not to be financially feasible to move it. Today it is a silent reminder of the former townsite. The old Zaring Warehouse had stood across the street and was razed so the salvaged materials could be used to construct a building replacing the lost cement grain elevator.

Mr. Dillie said, "After the bulk of the moving crew left to do other moving chores, myself and Charlie Cotant, young an foolish and not afraid of heights, tied in the rafters and nailed down shelton sheeting on the rickety roof. Bob Ewing Sr. and I continued to work rebuilding and installing the grain distributing system in the top of the building. By harvest time, we had everything working and ready for the new 1926 wheat crop.

"The one brick building restored exactly as it had been in the old town was the Methodist Church building. The old auditorium, a massive shell, presented a moving problem.

"The most difficult building to move was the Grand Hotel; it actually broke several moving outfits. For a long time, the building stood on the brink of the railroad cut, approximately where the overpass is now. Eventually, it was lowered into the cut and then jacked up and out again.

"For several years we were kept busy repairing homes. Homes without basements, were later excavated using a scraper or a Farmall tractor. Basement walls were built out of handmade cement blocks and covered with a coat of plaster."[42]

---

[42] March 31, 1966, Power County Press

# CHAPTER FIFTEEN

# MORE ON THE IRRIGATION STORY

Mr. Perrine remained actively involved planning the irrigation system from Shelly to Raft River. His involvement ended with the sale of the Southern Idaho Water Power Company to the Idaho Power Company.

The Power County Irrigation District had originally organized to promote the irrigation of land at Neeley where landowners had contemplated obtaining water from Fort Hall through a canal. Moench, an engineer, had laid out an elaborate system of canals which would have been successful except during drought years. The drought years of 1924 and 1926 showed that his Fort Hall canal system could not provide adequate water without a dam at American Falls.

The best solution for Neeley would be installation of a 36 inch penstock into the new Dam. The Neeley landowners presented their proposal and it was accepted. They purchased a 36 inch penstock at a cost of $1,265.75 and paid $42,000 for a pumping station to lift water through 53,000 feet of steel pipe to irrigate 4000 acres of vacant, sagebrush land at Neeley.

Even the penstock proved inadequate to cope with the severe drought of 1930 to 1934. Nevertheless, without the cooperation of the Bureau of Reclamation during the construction of the $6,000,000 dam, this small irrigation project would not have been possible.[43]

Going back in history, the Riverside Addition became part of the new incorporated town in 1907. A levy was then assessed, the moneys collected to place a pipe inside the future dam for irrigation purpose, along with contributions from the American Falls Natatorium Company.

Michaud Flats got its name in the 1840's from a Hudson Bay French fur trading scout, Michaud La Claire who worked in the Fort Hall area. The Fort Hall Bottoms' was an especially rich area envied

---

[43] Saga of American Falls Dam by I.E. Irvin

for its abundant wild grasses and wildlife. White settlers began to claim this land in 1860.

In 1913, Idaho Senator, James L. Brady, promised to accomplish the watering of Michaud Flats, the land between Pocatello and American Falls.

Early 1900, various small irrigation projects up and down the river began to interest local people in the possibilities of irrigation. They petitioned the county commissioners to investigate the possibilities of irrigating the Michaud area. Frank Moench, the private engineer brought in to make tests and to survey, submitted a plan using a canal system from Michaud to below Neeley.

The cost of the Moench Plan was placed at $200,000. Unfortunately, before the project was funded, a severe drought year, in 1919, proved that using Mr. Moench's Plan would not provide enough water to sustain a viable system at times of greatest need. The Moench Plan was abandoned.

However, the 1919 drought did point out the critical need for a large water storage system. Later, the resemblance of his proposed plan to the present one is remarkable. Mr. Moench had indicated a reservoir shore line of 125 miles which is almost exactly the same as the one submitted later to Congress for the dam at American Falls. Frank Moench nearly succeeded in achieving the same thing with much less technology.

The Michaud Flats Project represents much struggle and dedication to become a green dream reality. To resurrect the 1900 Moench idea, in 1939, the Power County Irrigation District formed to find way to allocate 420,000 acre feet of water, for local use, using water from a proposed South Fork Reservoir. In addition, they wanted 70,000 feet from American Falls Reservoir. It was not a good time because Europe and Asia were exhibiting warlike attitudes. In 1940, the Great World War rearranged priorities again.

Committee member, William Hess, made a visit to Washington D.C. in an effort to recapture necessary funding.

The Corp. of Engineers reported that the Palisades Project should be authorized because it would not only benefit agriculture but also provide power for defense plants being built in Utah. The Government refused to fund it.

February 10, 1947, the now disbanded water district met to reform

as *The Power County Irrigation Committee*. This water district had

the responsibility of making arrangements for construction of the

Michaud Flats Project.

Both landowners and the Indian Service voted 100% to support

Judge Baum to hire an engineer to estimate costs. A conflict arose

when potential users upstream fought to block use of water for the

Michaud area. At this point the Pocatello Chamber proposed that

they be included because together the Committee and the Chamber

together would be able to assure early completion of the Palisades

Project.

The Power County Irrigation Committee resulted from the

merging of Martin Canal Company and Woodville Canal Company.

February 20, 1949, representatives for all the irrigation districts

met. These included:

Twin Falls Canal Company, North Side Canal Company, New

Sweden Canal Company, Aberdeen-Springfiled Canal Company, Fort

Hall Water User's Association, The Indian Agency, and the Power

County Irrigation Committee. They met to express concern about return water flow, allocation, and distribution rights.[44]

Finally, Senator Frank Church submitted a Bill, attached to an Amendment. In this way funds were increased by $1,000,000.

After many years of struggle to achieve funding for an irrigation system, in 1954, Congress authorized the Michaud Flats Irrigation project from Fort Hall to Eagle Rock eight miles south of American Falls. The plan involved lifting stored water for distribution by electrically powered pumps to supply 65000 acres. Well water from underground sources would supply an additional 4,630 acres.

---

[44] Power County Press

# CHAPTER SIXTEEN

# MORE ON THE DAM STORY, circa 1977

State Senator Joe Allen appealed to Congress 'to stop procrastinating on the reconstruction of the American Falls Dam.' He pointed out, 'The highway commission already has contributed one million towards constructing a four lane highway on the new dam.'

'For the past seven years a diligent group from American Falls and Aberdeen have worked to achieve a safe crossing. We have corresponded with all Congressional delegates. We have met with the State Highway Department and the Bureau of Reclamation.'

'Lives have been lost because of the narrow roadway. Daily those, who must use this dangerous crossing, have their lives threatened.

'Respectfully we request a joint bipartisan effort... to act in favor of this urgent matter.'[45]

---

[45] Sept. 28, 1972... Power County Press

A guided tour of the 1927 dam revealed the importance of replacing the old crumbling structure. Water had begun to seep underneath the dam. Everett Browser, a site inspector, said, "The concrete has deteriorated to such a point I doubt the structure would have lasted another five years."

Even this repair brought opposition from Twin Falls farmers who claim it is not necessary at this time. Some were still paying on the former dam; they were in the minority, though. When it was learned that Idaho Power Company would pay a large portion of the new costs, the Twin falls resistance subsided.

When it was learned a long delay would be involved if the project were federally funded, Bonding was arranged; to avoid a tax penalty, a special Bill was passed through Congress. Work on the new construction began when most of the problems had been settled.[46]

50 years after finishing the dam, in 1927, the crumbling, partially unsafe structure was repaired with the expected cost to be $38,000,000. In 1975, a new traffic bridge was built below the dam before actual work on the dam itself could begin because all traffic on

---

[46] 1975 Power County Press

the old dam roadway would be stopped, permanently, with exception of construction vehicles.

Construction on the dam began February 1976. Engineers removed the main spillway section in September 1977. The old spillway was left intact for flood protection.

All the work was completed by December.

A visitor would be struck by the immensity of the project. Speech almost impossible with workers operating jackhammers, drills and large trucks communicating using hand signals.

Everett Bowser, an on-site inspector, explained the entire operation as extremely complicated. Ninety men worked on various phases of the operation. Men drilling bedrock were highest paid at $10.00 per hour. Other workers received $3.60. Each day, one thousand yards of concrete was poured until December.

Spillways remained intact until September when water was diverted to the newer section, allowing removal of a section of the old spillway. Excavation of the right abutment and reconstruction with final completion projected to be December 1977.[47]

[47] August 1976... Power County Press

# CHAPTER SEVENTEEN

# SCHOOLS AND EDUCATION

For short terms, public school in American Falls had been held in a one-room log house near the river bank. By 1899, a neat cut-stone school building had been erected close to the railroad known as Washington School. A smaller wooden structure housed the Lincoln Elementary School. When the town relocated, the Lincoln name transferred to the new school in the new town site.

An article found in one of the early American Falls newspapers, in 1899, referred to a visit by students from Albion State Normal School. The following is a report, apparently written by one of the Albion students:

"...coming from The Albion Normal School, we naturally did not expect much in the way of schools. We found ourselves agreeably surprised at the splendid rock building, so well furnished and filled with many bright faces of boys and girls.

144

"If American Falls does not have the services of Mrs. Washburn another session, it will be the town's loss. We prophesy great things for her in her profession. She has the tact to educate, and the ability of drawing out the best in a pupil. Evidently she has the natural love for the work of teaching."

"What is still more surprising... the pupils are advanced. The teacher, Mrs. Washburn, is not a stern, domineer, but an attractive lady ruling by the law of kindness. What is most delightful and seldom realized is that all parents speak well of her and all pupils are attached to their teacher."[48]

During this era there were many small one room schools. To name a few: *Pleasant Valley, Sunny Valley, Quigley, Mt. Hope, Fairview, Prosperity, Landing, Washington, Williams, Lake Channel, Ringe, Neeley, Landing, Mountain View, Fall Creek, Cove, Cold Creek, Warm Creek, Eliason, Excaliber, Central, East Fork, Roy,*

---

[48] February 2, 1899... The Falls Power

*** American Falls Boomerang was a competitor Newspaper...

*Greentop, Lyons, Valley view, Bannock Center, Meadow, Pauline, Crystal, Sun Beam, Garns, Borah, Coolidge, Cedar Creek, McKinley, Cedar Ridge, Washington, and Lincoln.*

May Williams taught the first school classes in Pleasant Valley in a homesteaders shack. In Pleasant Valley, the majority of the settlers came from Eastern European countries. Few spoke English and even fewer teachers spoke anything except English.

At this time, teachers were usually young and were prohibited from marrying. The one room schools seldom had living quarters so the teacher would often take turns living with the student's families. Accommodations were often less than desirable given the crowded conditions the families themselves were living under.

Not only was the teacher expected to help at the host home but at school, the teacher had many duties. A teacher was required to start the fire, carry out the ashes, sweep and mop out at the school before the children arrived. Some school boards might work out an arrangement to assist the teacher by supplying the water and coal.

A few of the country schools provided a barn to protect the horses used by the children. Schools did not necessarily provide buses and if they did, it was apt to be one of the older students who drove an open wagon.

Fairview School was one of the largest in the county having two rooms and two teachers for the eight grades. All the other county schools had one teacher for eight grades.

Many of these school had a short life history while others were still in use as late as 1950. Few still operate today[49, 50]

When the original town had to be moved to make way for dam construction, it meant building a new school.

The Washington School, an impressive stone building constructed before 1899, had been the High School. The new school building was intended to house both elementary and high school students. It was named Lincoln in honor of the school being lost at the former townsite. The new Lincoln School had a capacity of 328 students.

---

[49] Power County Court House Records

[50] Main Street American Falls

During construction, Ernest White & Company encountered a lot of rock which challenged their progress increasing the cost to $110,000. Pouring of foundations, though, proceeded without much delay. Dedication of the new building took place on Friday January 8, 1925.[51, 52]

Very soon, though, the school building was too small. Many of the country schools consolidated or closed. This meant students were now being sent to American Falls. The Washington School could not accommodate them all and, for a time, the new high school building accepted elementary students to relieve the overcrowding.

Upon completion of the new High School, the Lincoln School building became the elementary school with the seventh and eighth grade students on the second floor. For a time, the entire building was used for the Junior High students. the building was removed to make way for other projects.

---

[51] January 17, 1924 American Falls Press

[52] January 8, 1925 American Falls Press

Construction of a new high school was completed in 1934. The new American Falls High School included a stage, gymnasium with bleachers, tennis courts, and track.[53]

The school was considered quite grand and to have teaching position here was indeed a privilege. One former teacher, shared her memories of that first year, "…in this wonderful new school building that had just every new thing possible.

"It had been both an exciting year and a difficult one for me because that year both parents had died leaving me alone to cope both with grief and the stress of being a new graduate, my first position.

At age 92, Jessie Stacey <u>Hutchison</u> Smith, one of the first teachers to teach at the new high school expressed how difficult her first year of teaching had been, in 1934. "Not because of teaching but because of personal problems. I taught History, Biology, Civics, Art and Girls Basketball. It was a wonderful year filled with unforgettable memories."

---

[53] 1934 American Falls Press

"I boarded with a young couple who lived in an Idaho Power Company house located below the dam. I loved the river. I will always remember the roar of the water when the gates were opened in the spring.

"I loved the town, too, and especially the town slogan, *"The Best Town by a Damsite"!*

"When I was hired to teach, in 1934, at the new American Falls High School, it truly was a beautiful building... a show place! The principal was Giff Davison, a stocky man with broad shoulders. He had a presence! When he walked through Study Hall, even though the boys had been causing me difficulties, it was absolutely quiet. I was to have coached the girls basketball team but Giff Davison assumed the job making me his assistant. He turned out a good team that year.

"Jay Nichols, a character, coached the boys team and at every game his dog was there at his side, can't remember the breed, though.

"I enjoyed so many of the students, wish I could remember all of their names but many years have passed since I taught in American

Falls." She paused thoughtfully, "There were several Rasts, Volmers, Mehlhaffs Zarings, and Basques, — Aguirre and Echevarria. Some of the students took joy in causing me grief.

"John Echevarria was always busy keeping things active in the classroom and in Study Hall. Years later, he was one of ten people awarded the Carnegie Medal for an act of bravery that year. I don't remember the details but he saved someone from drowning near the power plant.

"Another student, Joe Zaring, a very brilliant boy who went on to University of Idaho; he distinguished himself by having gotten the highest grade point and honors of any student ever to attend University!

"Another exciting memory was, in 1935, when U.S. senator William E. Borah dedicated the new American Falls High School. As a young new teacher, to be in the presence of such an important dignitary was one really big moment for me!

"The school had a wonderful marching band and they looked so smart in their new red uniforms with gold buttons and braids. This band put American Falls on the music map by earning national recognition for excellence. In 1936, the band was invited to Portland, Oregon for the 'Rose Parade' where they again won first place as well as the hearts the people. This was quite remarkable considering the size of the community.[54]

Jessie had been invited to the 2000 year *All School Reunion.* She had eagerly accepted. With considerable anticipation, she looked forward to seeing some of her former students. Unfortunately, sudden health problems prevented her presence.

---

[54] Personal Interview with Jessie Hutchison Smith… by Ella Rast

Panoramic views of American Falls City

1903, 1925 during constrution and 1976 after repair and restoration

The first two Power Plant

Original Town Scene: Remington Hotel, Winter view of time,
Fall Creek Sheep Company—'selling out'

Raising the Corner Stone 1925

The Corner Stone

**NUMEROUS TRACKS** for construction cranes can be seen atop the partially constructed American Falls dam in the early 1920's. The photo shows the dam in a phase where it is just starting to reach out over the river with two construction cranes busily at work on the right hand side.

1926. DAM CONSTRUCTION BEGINS.

GRADING FOR THE BUSINESS DISTRICT. IF FOR RESIDENTIAL AREA,
WEEDS & SAGEBRUSH GREW BACK BEFORE HOUSES WERE MOVED.

Erecting south wing of right wall

Penstock connections for power

Outlet opening facing upstream

Bird's eye view of coffer dam and the old wooden bridge

Roosevelt Street

New water in new town, Tom Sparks

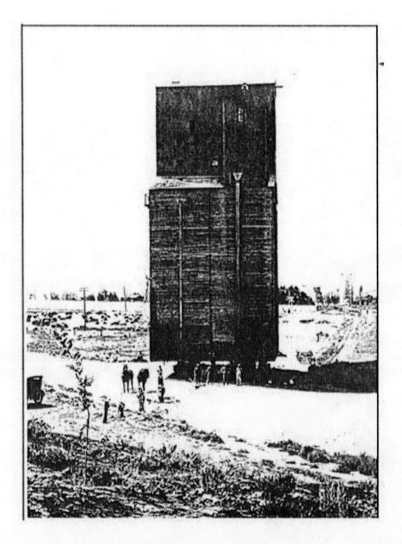

Grain Elevator on the move

Town going under water

St John's Lutheran Church on wheels

House being moved by a tractor

NO.27. AMERICAK FALLS DAM AND RAILROAD, BRIDGE, AMERICAM FALLS IDA

1927 - THE TOWN IS MOVED. SOME AREAS OF THE OLD TOWN WERE ON HIGH GROUND AND DIDN'T HAVE TO BE MOVED. THE DAM IS COMPLETED

CIRCA 1930. A LOW WATER YEAR REVEALING PARTS OF ORIGINAL TOWN - NOTE CAR BODY AT L HAND MARGIN. SITE

Contrasts. Proud new dam and a devastated old town site

Houses on new lots

Looking down Polk Street

A view down new Main Street

1927 third Power plant in operation

Third Plant after completion.

The Falls before the First Hydroelectric Plant
Area after the Dam
Construction of third Plant

An aerial view of the dam taken in 2002

# BIBLIOGRAPHY

The American Falls Boomerang

The Falls Power                           February 2, 1899

The American Falls Advertiser

The American Falls Advertiser

American Falls Press

Rockland Times

Power County Booster

The Power County Press

Power Press                 Emiliy Jomes          April 30, 2001

Idaho State Journal

New York Herald

Salt Lake Tribune           O.A. Fitzgerald       July 13, 1925

Duluth Herald                                     October 25, 1923

Idaho State Journal         Bertha Sawyer

'Saga of the American       Irvin Rockwell

Falls Dam

'Memories of the Town       Power County Press     July 16, 1980

Beneath the Waters.'

'In Mountain Shadows'          Carlos Santos

The Journal of                    Timothe Lemperi        1848

'Drowned Memores'      Minerva Kohlhepp Teichert        approx. 1927

'Legacy of Light' a history of Idaho Power Company        Susan Stacy

'Anatomy of the          Ralph W. Maughan          Idaho State Univ. Press

Snake River Plain'

'Sometimes Dreams Come True'      O. Bert Baum

'Across the Rockies to the Columbia      John Kirk Townsend        1834

'Main Street American Falls      Am Falls Chamber of Commerce      1980

Idaho, 1890-1990'

Essay and photos                  Nancy Sparks Lawrence

'Tales of Eastern Idaho'          David Crowder

'The Story of Idaho'              Virgil M Young          1990

'We Sagebrush Folks'              Annie Pike Greenwood

'Idaho Handbook''                 Don Root                1992

'Celebrate Idaho, Idaho's Ethinic Heritage'    Mary Reed

'Idaho of Yesterday'              Thomas Donaldson

'Idaho Story'                     Betty Derig

"Rocks, Rails, & Trails'      Paul Link & Chilton Phoenix      1994

'Idaho Yesterday and Today,'      A collection of essays

'Historical Sketch of Power

'Welcome to Main Street American Falls Idaho' American Falls Chamber of Commerce

| | | |
|---|---|---|
| Exploring Idaho Geology | Terry Maley | 1987 |
| Roots of the American Falls Stake | Maril & Julia Beck | 1982 |
| Bridges on the River Snake | H. F. Gambil | 1975 |
| Historical Edition Power County PressDoroty | Dorothy S. Chandler | 1937 |

# ABOUT THE AUTHOR

I am a member of the Idaho Writer's league, participate in writing groups through Idaho State University and hold membership in the Power County Historical Society.

My writing instructor, Dee Lopez of Portland, Oregon, taught at Mt. Hood Community College. Without her stern encouragement and insistence that I keep writing, I might not have finished my father's story and my first book, *I Remember That Good Yet...*, how a 1922 Russian immigrant to Idaho who found life on the desert harder than in Russia.

I attended a one-room country school, Mt. Hope School, where we were taught learning skills. It was stressed that "graduation is not the end of your education, it means you are finally ready to begin learning for the rest of your life".

After graduation from American Falls High School, I entered Emanuel Nursing School in Portland, Oregon. Some years later, a B.S. Degree was granted by Linfield College. I continued to pursue a career in nursing until 1993. With my children grown, I left Oregon to retire in Idaho with time to write and paint.